QUICK AND NATURAL RICE DISHES

QUICK

AND NATURAL

Rice Dishes

The 75 Most Popular Recipes from

20 Years of East West

Natural Health

From the Editors of East West/Natural Health Magazine

East West/Natural Health Books

East West/Natural Health Books
17 Station Street
Brookline, Massachusetts 02146

ISBN 0-936184-12-4

Published in the United States of America

First Edition

135798642

Distributed to the natural foods trade by East West/Natural Health Books, 17 Station Street, Brookline, MA 02146 and to the book trade by The Talman Company, 131 Spring St., #201E-N, New York, NY 10012.

Cover and text design by Sara Eisenman
Illustrations by Leah Palmer Preiss

Acknowledgments

Special thanks to recipe tester Daphne Rota, cookbook editor Linda Elliot, and designer Sara Eisenman for their considerable talent and expertise in shaping this book. Many thanks are also due to the chefs and cooks who over the past twenty years have contributed to *East West/Natural Health* the recipes that make up the bulk of this book: Karen Acuff, Akiko Aoyagi, Indira Balkissoon, Karen Stein Bard, Jan Belleme, John Belleme, Susan Carskadon, Annemarie Colbin, Wendy Esko, Mary Estella, Neil Garland, Barbara Jacobs, Aveline Kushi, Nam-Ye Lee, Ron Lemire, John Lewallen, Joan Livingston, Meredith McCarty, Lauren McGuinn, Isobel O'Donnell, Brother Ron Pickarski, Ann Rawley, Daphne Rota, Kathryn Silver, Eric Stapleman, Pieter Steneker, and Rebecca Wood.

Contents

CHAPTER THREE: ONE-DISH MEALS

CHAPTER FOUR: RICE AND...

Introduction:
The Amazing Grain

Rice is arguably the world's most important food. It is the second most widely cultivated cereal in the world, after wheat, and accounts for the bulk of the diet for half the world's population. In much of Asia rice is so central to the culture that the word is almost synonymous with food. In Chinese the line in the Lord's Prayer is translated as "give us this day our daily rice," and a Japanese proverb states that "A meal without rice is no meal."

The attributes that have long attracted Asians to this grain are now becoming more well known to North Americans. Fans of rice cite its ease of preparation, its flexibility (it can be either a main or a minor ingredient in everything from soups to entrées to desserts), and its ability to absorb flavors while retaining its texture. Because it's also nutritious and economical, rice is being hailed as "the pasta of the '90s." Its rising popularity in the West coincides with an increasing number of types and varieties being marketed. Well-stocked supermarkets and natural foods stores now offer over a dozen distinct rices, from short grain sweet brown to foreign aromatics such as basmati to hearty new domestically developed varieties such as Wehani.

Though a relatively late import to the West, rice (*Oryza sativa*) has a long and colorful history. One of the oldest cultivated grains, it is not known where it originated, though it was probably first grown in Southeast Asia. The earliest record of rice production in China goes back some 5,000 years. It was the Chinese who discovered that rice yields could be increased considerably if fields were kept flooded. Rice flourishes underwater because of the plant's ability to transport oxygen from leaves to submerged roots, and because flooding during most or all of the growing season helps to minimize weed competition.

Rice made its way to Japan about 1000 B.C. and then spread to the Middle East. The first Western contact with rice was circa 326 B.C. when

Alexander the Great's soldiers saw rice fields in India and brought the grain back to Greece. The Moors introduced the crop to Spain around 700 A.D. The Spaniards took it to Italy in 1400 and then to their West Indies colonies in the early 1600s. Some of the earliest English settlers of Virginia brought rice to North America in 1647. It didn't begin to flourish as a crop in the U.S., however, until it was introduced to South Carolina some 40 years later. By the beginning of the 18th century the U.S. was a rice exporter, sending shipments to England and Europe. After the Civil War rice cultivation in America shifted west, first to Louisiana and the states of the Mississippi Valley and then, in the first decade of the 20th century, to California.

A member of the grass family, rice is commonly thought to be tropical and equatorial, but it also grows in temperate zones and is now cultivated not only in Asia but in parts of Latin America, Africa, and Europe. Some of the largest rice producers outside Asia include Egypt, Italy, Spain, and Brazil. Today the U.S. is the world's top exporter of rice, though it accounts for only 2 percent of the world's annual production of about one trillion pounds.

The quintessential local food, half of all rice is consumed within eight miles of where it is grown. Some Asian populations consume it at a per capita rate of 200-500 pounds per year, counting on it for 30-70 percent of total calories. Though it is increasingly popular in U.S., per capita consumption here is on the order of a comparatively meager 12 pounds per year.

A NUTRITIONAL POWERHOUSE

Depending primarily upon the type of processing it has undergone, rice ranks high on the list of most nutritious foods. Whole (brown) rice provides significant levels of fiber, complex carbohydrates, some of the B vitamins and vitamin E, and the minerals calcium, iron, phosphorus, and potassium. It has most of the essential amino acids, although it is low in lysine. Traditionally it has been eaten with beans or a complementary legume to be a reliable source of protein. Another nutritional advantage is that fewer people are allergic to rice than to wheat or most other grains.

Since rice has no cholesterol, only a trace of fat, and provides about 160 calories per cooked cup, it is not surprising that it is the backbone of a successful weight-loss regimen, the "rice diet." Developed by Dr. Walter Kempner of the Duke University Medical Center in the late 1930s, the rice diet has improved the health of many thousands of people over the past 50 years. The rice diet enjoyed a recent spurt of popularity when it became the subject of a bestselling book, *The Rice Diet Report*, in the mid-'80s. Kempner's rice diet is low in protein, salt, cholesterol, and fat yet high in complex carbohydrates and fiber. Since it emphasizes fresh vegetables and fruit along with rice, the diet is consistent with the basic nutritional recommendations now being made by the federal government and progressive nutritionists.

Researchers have recently uncovered a new and potentially dramatic nutritional benefit for rice. Experiments show that the oil in rice bran may be unique in how it affects blood cholesterol levels. It appears that consuming rice bran oil has the effect of keeping at an even level the body's "good" high-density lipoprotein (HDL) cholesterol, while simultaneously lowering the "bad" low-density lipoprotein (LDL) that encourages hardening of the arteries and heart disease. The components of rice bran oil that may be responsible for these effects are substances called unsaponifiable oils, or those that do not convert to soaps, in this case a potentially harmful occurrence

A RAINBOW OF RICES

To distinguish among rices, it is necessary to know something about rice processing, grain size, and common varieties.

PROCESSING. In the U.S. as in the rest of the world, some 98 percent of all rice for direct consumption is milled and polished until it is white, to make it easier to store, cook, and digest. Such processing has been done since ancient times, even in traditional societies such as those in China, India, and Japan. Until about the 19th century, however, it was a labor-intensive process to hand-mill rice. Thus, white rice became associated with wealth and privilege, and brown with poverty. When mechanization brought cheaper milled rice to virtually everyone, brown rice quickly became a rarity throughout the world. Only within the past twenty years have natural foods advocates and health activists helped to re-establish the importance of whole grains such as brown rice.

Rice direct from the field is called rough or paddy rice and has a hard outer hull or husk around the grain. The first step in the milling process removes the hull. The remaining kernel is called whole or brown rice. It includes several outer bran layers that encase the starchy white endosperm and the small germ or embryo that rests at the base of the endosperm. During the subsequent milling steps, gradual abrasive action strips away the bran layers and some of the endosperm, including the germ, leaving white rice. The outer parts of the kernel house much of the vitamins and minerals in rice, so the waste byproduct is sold for cattle feed and the manufacture of vitamin concentrates.

Though it is not often done, rice can be milled in degrees between whole grain brown and white. Such "beige" or "partially milled" rice has the advantage of retaining much of the fiber, nutrients, and protein of brown rice, otherwise lost in the transition to white rice, while offering quicker cooking, better storage, and a lighter tasting product than brown rice.

Almost all rice for human consumption, however, is milled all the way to white. At that point rice is usually further processed by passing it through machines that polish it by removing any flour adhering to the grain. Broken or fragmented kernels are separated out, to be used by brewers or rice flour manufacturers. The whole polished rice is then sometimes treated with calcium carbonate to make it white and glucose to make it sweet.

Since most of the nutrients have been removed in the journey from brown to white rice, rice produced in the U.S. is usually enriched by being soaked in a solution of vitamins and minerals. White rice imported to the U.S. typically is not enriched.

One method for preventing the wholesale loss of nutrients during refining is parboiling. Unhulled rice is soaked and then steamed under pressure, which drives the water-soluble nutrients of the bran into the endosperm where they are preserved during milling. Such "converted" or "pretreated" rice yields separate, fluffy grains when cooked.

Rice processing of course is not limited to milling and polishing. Rice flakes, for instance, are made from long grain brown rice that is steamed, flattened by steel rollers, and dried in an oven. This process also shortens cooking time but keeps nutrients. There are also a number of innovative new packaged rice products on the market, such as quick brown rice, puffed rice, and the ubiquitous rice cakes.

GRAIN SIZE. The three common grain sizes are short, medium, and long. Short grain varieties are usually grown in more temperate climates than medium and long grain varieties. Short grain rice is sometimes called pearl or round rice and has plump kernels that are moist and sticky when cooked. Medium grain and long grain rices tend to separate when cooked and to cook up drier and more fluffy.

In general long grain varieties are more popular than short grain varieties in the U.S. Nutritionally there's only marginal differences among the grain sizes.

Processing characteristics are more distinctive. Short grain rice works well for puffing, medium grain rice for dry breakfast cereals and baby foods, and long grain rice for parboiling, in canned soups, and in quick-cooking products.

VARIETIES. Scientists classify rice into two broad categories. The first is the subspecies *indica*, characterized by tall, tropical plants that bear long and slender grains. The second is the subspecies *japonica*, which grow better in more temperate climates and yield shorter, rounder, more glutinous grain. There is much variety within each of these subspecies.

One type of rice is termed sweet rice, and is usually a short-grained variety. It contains slightly more protein than other varieties, is sticky when cooked, and is most often used for desserts, puddings, and so forth.

Aromatic rices form another class, characterized by a distinctive nutty aroma and taste. The most popular aromatics are imports such as basmati, a flavorful and light long grain rice grown primarily in the foothills of the Himalayas, and jasmine from Thailand. After basmati is harvested in India and Pakistan it is allowed to age for several years, which dries it and intensifies its flavor. True Indian basmati and most other foreign aromatics are available in the U.S. chiefly in their milled, white form.

Within the past few years, however, a number of American rice growers have developed domestic aromatic varieties, most of which are available unmilled. For instance, Wehani is a hearty, russet-colored aromatic developed and grown by the organic rice producer Lundberg Family Farms of Richvale, California. Wehani is a long grain with a red bran layer. Lundberg has also developed a lighter aromatic brown called Royal, as well as a few other special rices such as a black rice called Japonica and a red short grain.

Another distinctive American rice grower is the Texmati Rice company of Alvin, Texas. Their Texmati brand rice is a domestically grown aromatic that's available not only in white and brown forms, but as "Lite Bran," a partially milled product with only a small portion of the bran removed. Texmati rice was produced by crossing basmati with a long grain rice. The company also markets a domestic white basmati they call Jasmati.

Finally, there is wild rice, which is actually not a rice but the seed of an aquatic grass (*Zizania aquatica*). In the wild it grows in shallow bodies of water in the lake region of Minnesota, Wisconsin, and Canada. Within the past ten years the commercial wild rice industry has moved to California, where the plant is cultivated in paddies and mechanically harvested. Traditional wild rice, often still hand-harvested by Native Americans, is becoming harder to find. Connoisseurs say that the difference, in taste and texture, makes the search for wild wild rice worth the effort. Look for "lake-harvested" or "hand-harvested" on the package. Paddy rice is often dark, almost black, and uniform in size and color, whereas lake rice is more varied, with grains being gray, green, brown, or red, sometimes even in same package.

Cooking time can vary for wild rices. Traditional lake rice may cook in 30 minutes or so, while paddy rices often take 45-60 minutes.

IS IT ORGANIC?

A final distinction among rices is whether the grain has been grown organically. Most domestic rice is grown on large, mechanized farms that use synthetic fertilizers, herbicides such as propanil and molinate to kill weeds, and pesticides to kill the rice water weevil and other "problem insects." The rice is usually then stored in massive silos where it is regularly fumigated with chemicals to kill molds and pests.

Organic growers, on the other hand, enrich soil by rotating crops or planting winter cover crops. Herbicides and pesticides are shunned in favor of natural methods to control weeds and insects, and carbon dioxide rather than strong fumigants is used in storage silos. Organic farmers may also try to keep rice in its unhulled state as long as possible, since removing the hull exposes the outer bran layers to oxygen and thus promotes rancidity.

A small but growing number of farmers in the U.S., such as the Lundbergs, are now following such organic methods and supplying high quality organic rice to supermarkets and natural foods stores around the country. Such organic brands are more expensive than conventionally grown rice, but many people who eat a lot of the grain feel it is well worth the price, both for nutritional and environmental reasons.

Consumers today are more protected against false claims about organic produce than they were ten years ago. Federal and state laws are more explicit about what it means for a crop to be grown organically, and a number of private companies now certify foods as organic. Look for such proof of certification on package labels or bulk bins.

When buying rice, whether organically or conventionally grown, look for clean, uniform grains without many green, immature, scratched, or broken grains, or any weed seeds, husks, or dirt. You can also smell the rice for the fresh pleasant smell of recently hulled rice.

TOOLS OF THE RICE CHEF

Rice can be cooked in a variety of ways, including boiling, baking, roasting, frying, and pressure-cooking. Pressure cooking offers a number of advantages over most other methods, including quickness of cooking. More importantly, with pot-boiling, as soon as steam builds up it is released even with a cover on, so you need to use enough water to allow for the loss. And with the escaping steam go flavor and nutrition, in the form of heat-sensitive and water-soluble vitamins. In a pressure cooker, air is expelled from the pot, steam is sealed in, and foods are bathed in pure steam, allowing them to retain nutrients, flavors, and aroma otherwise lost in vapor. The flavor and texture of pot-boiled brown rice are rather dull and dry compared to the richness of pressure cooked. (White

6

rice, whether regular or aromatic, doesn't cook well in a pressure cooker.)

Many good pressure cookers are on the market now, due to a resurgence of interest in healthful cooking and saving time. They are sleek, state-of-the-art pots with names like Chantal, Cuisinart, Kuhn-Rikon, and Aeturnum, and dependable workhorses like Presto. Although they all work on the same simple principle, operation and features vary. Shop around, talk to friends who have them, and try to determine which model would suit you best. Sizes range from two- to twenty-quart capacity, with four-, six-, and eight-quart in the family size range. Pressure cooker manufacturers advise never filling the cooker more than two-thirds full—which will help you decide which capacity to choose.

Pressure cookers come in aluminum, stainless steel, and enamel (glass fused to metal). Aluminum is the cheapest, but not worth the cost saving since the metal can react with foods and cause off-flavors. Enamel is wonderful but expensive. A heavier pot is better than a light one, even though it may cost more. It will last longer, heat more evenly, and cause less scorching. With occasional replacement of sealing rings and vents, through manufacturer or hardware stores, a quality pot may last a lifetime.

Pressure cooking is good for many foods but not so good for others, particularly those (such as split peas, oatmeal, and others) that may clog the air-release vent or valve. The manufacturer's instructions will list such foods and should be read carefully.

A useful accompaniment to a pressure cooker is the item known variously as a heat diffuser, flame spreader, or flame tamer. It is simply a metal or asbestos disc with a handle attached. It slips under a pot to prevent scorching during long, slow cooking. Several recipes in this book will tell you to bring the pot up to pressure, then reduce heat and place a flame tamer under. It is handy for pot-boiling, too. If you have an electric stove, choose an appropriate flame tamer.

COOKING TIPS

The following chart provides a handy one-stop reference for pressure-cooking or pot-boiling various types of rice. See Chapter Two: Basics and Side Dishes for more complete cooking instructions for white aromatic rice and wild rice. Note that 1 cup of raw rice generally yields about 3 cups of cooked rice. Also, the amounts of water and cooking times are approximate and may vary with such factors as the particular variety of rice, its freshness, and whether you want drier or stickier grains. Other factors may include the type of stove and cookware. Also, if you're cooking more than two cups of rice the amount of water needed per cup decreases slightly.

TYPE OF RICE	PRESSURE COOKING	POT-BOILING
Long grain white	do not pressure cook	1 cup rice 2 cups water 15-20 minutes
Short grain brown	1 cup rice 1½ cups water 50 minutes	1 cup rice 2 cups water 50 minutes
Medium grain brown	1 cup rice 1½ cups water 45 minutes	1 cup rice 2 cups water 50 minutes
Long grain brown	1 cup rice 1½ cups water 45 minutes	1 cup rice 2 cups water 45 minutes
Sweet brown	1 cup rice 1½ cups water 45 minutes	1 cup rice 2 cups water 50 minutes
Partially milled	1 cup rice 1¾ cups water 15-20 minutes	1 cup rice 2 cups water 20 minutes
White aromatic	do not pressure cook	1 cup rice 2 cups water 15-20 minutes
Brown aromatic	1 cup rice 2¼ cups water 45 minutes	1 cup rice 2½ cups water 45 minutes
Wild rice	1 cup rice 1¾ cups water 45 minutes	1 cup rice 4 cups water 45 minutes

For most dishes the goal is to have cooked grains that remain separate, are a little firm (al dente) but not hard, and retain their flavor. Rice can absorb a great deal of liquid. You can soak it over night or for a few hours in water, milk, oil, or stock to soften grains. One special consideration is that cooking rice in a slightly acidic medium such as tomato sauce may require a little more liquid or a longer cooking time.

With all rices, rinse them well before cooking to wash away any dust and chaff. To do this, place measured rice into the cooking pot and fill it with cool water. Swish the rice around with your hand, and gently pour off the water. Repeat two or three times, and then pour through a fine mesh strainer to drain.

Place rice, measured water, and salt, if using, in the pot and afix lid. Bring up to pressure over high heat, then turn down, place flame tamer under the pot, and cook for the allotted time. (For pot-boiling, bring to a boil, then reduce heat and position the flame tamer.) When the rice is done, remove the pressure cooker from the burner even if you have turned off the flame, as the rice will continue to cook from the heat of the burner or flame detector. Also remove the rice from the pressure cooker as soon as the pressure is down. If allowed to sit, the moisture will cause the grains to expand, thus producing a wet and tasteless bowl of rice. Use a wet wooden paddle to remove the finished rice from the pot and place the rice in a bowl.

SERVING AND STORING RICE

Rice is best cooked immediately before serving, but if it must sit cover it with a cotton towel and a lid or bamboo mat. This allows the rice to cool slowly and prevents steam from falling back into the rice and making it mushy. Also, avoid stirring rice unless it is called for in the recipe. It can also make the grain too sticky.

Since the bran and polish contain about 85 percent of the oil in rice, brown rice can go rancid much more readily than white rice, especially during hot weather. Uncooked white rice will keep in a sealed container for a year or longer, but for brown it is best to buy relatively small quantities that you'll use up in three to six months. Purchase from a store with a good turnover, and keep the rice in a cool, dry, dark place in a sealed container. Uncooked rice can be kept in the refrigerator or freezer if you have room. If not, a few bay leaves in the container may help discourage grain moths.

If your kitchen stays cool over night during the winter you can leave cooked rice out, covered with a towel or rice mat, and it won't dry out as fast as it does in the refrigerator. Cooked rice can be kept in the refrigerator for up to about five days. After about three days, it may begin to "retrograde" or dry out. You can either scrape off the top, crusty layer and discard, or add a few tablespoons of moisture before reheating. A good place for leftover rice is a stir fry, soup, pie, or simply heated in a pan with a little water or vegetable stock.

In general any rice can be substituted for another, with a few exceptions such as it's usually best to use a sweeter short or medium grain rice for dessert dishes. In most of the following recipes, a specific variety is listed in the ingredients but you can substitute white for brown or vice versa, depending upon your tastes, mood, or whatever. Unmilled or partially milled rice is the more healthful choice for everyday eating but white also has its place.

Chapter One:
Appetizers and Soups

NORI PINWHEEL APPETIZERS

Makes 16 pieces

These pinwheels of contrasting color are lovely on an appetizer table. Making them may seem daunting at first, but it is really quite simple and enjoyable to do. Once you have it down you will be creating your own delectable combinations and amazing your friends with this Japanese specialty.

2 sheets toasted nori
1½ cups cooked rice, brown or white
1 scallion, cut into long slivers
1 tablespoon prepared mustard
1 tablespoon sauerkraut

To toast nori: hold the sheet by a corner over medium heat, moving it constantly or waving it gently until the color changes somewhat and it is fragrant and brittle.

Place the nori on a bamboo sushi mat (available at Oriental shops and well-stocked natural foods shops) and cover it with a thin layer of freshly cooked, preferably warm, rice three-fourths of the way down the sheet. Spread the mustard along a line about an inch from the bottom edge of the rice. Place the scallion slivers and the sauerkraut on top of the mustard. Roll the ingredients firmly, tucking the leading edge in (do not roll the mat into the sushi). Moisten the uncovered end of nori before completing the roll, to seal. Remove the mat altogether, and slice the roll into 8 pieces with a moistened sharp knife. Arrange attractively on a platter and garnish with carrot curls or chrysanthemum blossoms.

RICE ROLLS WITH CARROT AND PARSLEY

Another unusual party food—eye-catching and tasty.

1 medium-size carrot
1 tablespoon umeboshi plum paste
1 tablespoon water
1 tablespoon minced parsley
1 sheet nori
3 cups cooked brown rice

Cut the carrot first on the diagonal into thin slices then into thin julienne (matchstick) pieces. Steam the carrot for one minute, or just until bright orange. Combine the umeboshi paste and the water in a small bowl and mash with a fork to mix. Add carrots and the parsley, mix again, and set aside. Toast the nori as described in the previous recipe, for Nori Pinwheel Appetizers. Cut the nori in half with scissors, then across into ½ -inch strips.

Mix carrot-parsley mixture with the rice. Moisten your hands with water, scoop out about 3 tablespoonfuls of rice mixture, and shape an oblong about 2 inches long. Repeat with remaining rice mixture, then wrap a strip of nori around the center of each roll of rice, moistening the overlap to seal.

A yellow chrysanthemum makes the perfect garnish.

CHINESE FIRECRACKERS

Unbeknownst to many Westerners, there are other rice "products" besides the whole grain. Centuries ago in the Far East, people discovered how to make delicately sweet rice syrup and tangy brown rice vinegar. The two flavors in combination have come to be known as "sweet and sour"—a taste that will never go out of style.

This tofu dish is called firecrackers because of the hot pepper. You can adjust the seasoning from this mild version to the traditional Chinese volcano by adding more cayenne or dried chili pepper.

1 pound firm tofu, pressed briefly and cut into 1-inch cubes
2 cups oil for deep-frying
1 scallion, thinly sliced on the diagonal, for garnish

SWEET AND SOUR SAUCE

3 tablespoons natural soy sauce
2 tablespoons rice syrup
2 tablespoons brown rice vinegar
pinch cayenne powder, or one small dried red pepper, seeded and crushed
1 tablespoon kuzu (crush chunks with the back of a spoon before measuring) dissolved in ¼ cup water
¾ cup water

Heat oil over medium flame until a drop of flour and water batter sinks to the bottom and immediately rises to the surface (but it should not be so hot that it smokes). Add half the tofu cubes and fry, turning occasionally, until golden, about 10 minutes. Drain on paper. Repeat with the remaining tofu.

To make the sauce, combine all ingredients in a small saucepan and bring to a simmer over medium-low heat, stirring constantly. Cook briefly, stirring, until sauce has thickened and is transparent. Add fried tofu to heat through and coat with sauce. Garnish with chopped scallions to serve, accompanied by a little dishful of toothpicks.

RICE PAPER SPRING ROLLS WITH PEANUT-VINEGAR DIPPING SAUCE

Serves 4 as main dish, 12 as appetizer

Rice paper, an ingenious invention of the traditional cooks of Thailand, is similar to eggroll wrappers. The beauty of rice paper is that it doesn't need any cooking. You can make quick appetizers or a meal at a moment's notice with leftover cooked rice, tofu, ginger, a few fresh vegetables, cooked shrimp or fish,…and rice paper. The following combination can be a springboard for your imagination.

Look for rice paper wrappers and lime leaves at an Oriental market.

12 rice paper wrappers (round ones, about 7 inches in diameter)
12 lettuce leaves, washed, patted dry, and chopped fine
½-1 cup cooked rice
12 scallions, cut into 5-inch lengths
½ pound firm tofu, cut into strips ¼-inch wide
1 cup chopped cilantro
2 tablespoons peeled and minced fresh ginger
6 lime leaves, minced, or 1 teaspoon grated lime zest (optional)

The wrappers must be soaked in water to make them pliable, and once they are ready you must work quickly before they dry out again. So before you begin to soak the wrappers, have all ingredients prepared and at hand.

Place a wrapper into a pie plate filled with lukewarm water and let it soak just until it is pliable, 30-60 seconds. Remove it, lay it flat on a plate, and place a little of each ingredient in the center in a strip about 2 inches wide and 5 inches long. Fold in the edges at the ends of the filling (this keeps the filling in), and roll it up, eggroll style, making an envelope. The paper will seal itself. Soak each wrapper, fill, and roll up.

You can make these ahead of time, even a day in advance, but you must cover them tightly with plastic wrap to keep them from drying out.

Serve with a sauce, either the one that follows or one made from Green Curry Sauce (see page 70) diluted by half with brown rice vinegar.

PEANUT-VINEGAR DIPPING SAUCE

Makes about 1 cup

½ cup brown rice vinegar
¼ cup finely chopped roasted peanuts
½ small cucumber, peeled, seeded, and diced
1 tablespoon rice syrup
1-2 tablespoons natural soy sauce

Roast raw peanuts on a baking sheet in a preheated 350°F oven for 10-15 minutes or just until golden and fragrant. Combine all ingredients and serve in individual small bowls.

ROSEMARY SALMON PÂTÉ

Serves 10-12

This delicately flavored pâté is especially good on slices of French bread. Use a fish mold, if you have one, and garnish the turned-out pâté with sprigs of fresh rosemary and wedges of lemon or surround it with red leaf lettuce.

2 tablespoons extra virgin olive oil
2 cups finely chopped red onion
½ teaspoon sea salt
3 tablespoons chopped fresh rosemary leaves
1½ pounds salmon fillets
3½ cups fish stock or water
2 tablespoons mirin
2 tablespoons lemon juice
1½ tablespoons agar flakes
½ cup chopped black olives
1 cup cooked rice (any kind except sweet brown)

Heat the oil in a skillet over medium heat and add the onions. Sauté briefly and then add the salt and rosemary. Continue to sauté, stirring, and when the onions are translucent, lay the salmon fillets over them. Gently add 1 cup of the stock or water, along with the mirin. Bring to a boil, then turn down to simmer, cover, and let poach for 8-12 minutes, or just until fish is cooked through and flakes easily. Remove fish and onions from pan with a slotted spoon and process in a blender with ½ cup of stock or water. Turn heat under poaching liquid to high, add the lemon juice, and reduce it to a somewhat thick concentrate, about 10 minutes.

Pour the remaining 2 cups of stock or water into a saucepan and sprinkle on the agar flakes. Slowly bring to a boil, then turn down to simmer, and cook for 5 minutes or until agar is dissolved, stirring occasionally. In a bowl, combine salmon, poaching reduction, agar mixture, olives, and rice. Pour into a lightly oiled fish mold, loaf pan, or other dish, let cool, and set in the refrigerator for an hour or so.

To serve, loosen sides of pâté with a knife and turn out onto a platter.

WILD RICE, SHALLOT, AND
MUSHROOM SOUP

A thick soup with a tender texture and the rich flavor of shallots.

1 tablespoon extra virgin olive oil
3 cups diced shallots
1 teaspoon Herbamare seasoning
1 cup wild rice, washed well, presoaked for several hours, and drained
8 cups water or stock

1 tablespoon extra virgin olive oil
1 medium carrot, diced
3 cups sliced white mushrooms

1 tablespoon extra virgin olive oil
4 cups sliced mushrooms (2 cups white, 2 cups shiitake works well)
2 tablespoons umeboshi vinegar
1 tablespoon mirin
3 tablespoons lemon juice
½ teaspoon each: dried oregano, marjoram, thyme, and basil

Heat the first tablespoon of oil over medium heat in pot. Add the shallots and sauté until transparent, about 5 minutes. Add Herbamare, wild rice, and water. Bring to a boil, then reduce to simmer.

Place a skillet over medium heat and add the second tablespoon of oil. Add the carrot and the 3 cups of mushrooms, and sauté for 5 minutes. Remove from heat and process in a blender the carrot and mushrooms with enough liquid from the stock pot to purée. Add the purée to the stock pot.

Reheat the skillet, without cleaning, and add the last tablespoon of oil. Add the 4 cups of mushrooms, the umeboshi vinegar, mirin, lemon juice, and herbs. Cook over low heat until the mushrooms are tender and have released their juice. Using a slotted spoon, remove the mushrooms and add them to the simmering stock pot. Turn the heat under the skillet to medium-high and reduce the liquid, stirring frequently, to concentrate and thicken it slightly, about 5-7 minutes. Remove from heat and pour into the pot, scraping the skillet as clean as possible.

Simmer the soup for 20-30 more minutes, or until the wild rice is very tender. Garnish with chopped watercress or parsley.

CREAM OF RICE AND BROCCOLI SOUP

Serves 4-6

A perky soup to build a meal around.

1 tablespoon extra virgin olive oil
1 cup diced onions
1 tablespoon minced garlic
1 teaspoon Herbamare seasoning
¼ teaspoon white pepper
¼ teaspoon cayenne
¼ teaspoon cumin powder
1½ teaspoons dried basil, or 2 tablespoons chopped fresh basil
2 teaspoons white wine vinegar
6 cups water or stock
2¾ cups cooked brown rice
2 cups diced peeled broccoli stems
2 cups bite-size broccoli florets
½ teaspoon umeboshi vinegar

Heat the oil over medium heat in a four-quart pot. Add the onions and garlic and sauté for 3-5 minutes or just until the onions are translucent. Add the Herbamare, spices, herbs, white wine vinegar, and 4 cups of the water or stock. Place the rice in a blender with the remaining 2 cups water or stock and process until creamy.

Add creamed rice to the pot and bring to a boil. Reduce to simmer, add the broccoli stems, and cook for 5 minutes. Add broccoli florets and cook 2 minutes more, or just until the florets are tender but still bright green. Add the umeboshi vinegar and remove from heat. Serve with a colorful garnish like nasturtium blossoms (they are edible) or steamed carrot rounds.

O ZONI
(Mochi Soup)

Mochi is a delicious Japanese whole grain food made from sweet brown rice. The sweet rice is cooked and pounded, which breaks the grains and enhances the glutinous quality of this variety of rice. It is a rather daunting task to perform at home, but luckily various flavors of mochi are readily available at natural foods stores.

mochi, cut into 6 blocks, each about 2 inches by 2 inches
8 cups water
6-inch piece kombu
¼ cup bonito flakes
1 small-to-medium-size burdock root
1 large carrot
½ teaspoon sea salt
8-10 mushrooms, sliced
1 tablespoon mirin
3 scallions, cut into l-inch lengths
4 leaves Chinese cabbage, chopped (optional)
¼-⅓ cup mellow white miso

Preheat oven to 375°F. Cut the mochi blocks into bite-sized cubes, place them on a lightly oiled baking sheet, and bake until they are slightly browned and puffy, 30-40 minutes. The mochi should be crispy but not melted—watch carefully.

While the mochi is cooking, bring water and kombu to a boil, then remove kombu and reserve for another use (such as chopping and adding to another soup, a salad, or other dish). Add bonito flakes, remove pot from heat, and let sit for 1-2 minutes. Strain, pressing bonito to extract all the flavor, and discard the flakes. Wash and scrub burdock, cut into 2-inch-long julienne strips, and immediately place in cold water to prevent discoloration. Cut carrot similarly but a little thicker. Drain the burdock and add it to the stock along with the salt. Simmer 10-15 minutes, and add carrots and mushrooms. Simmer 10 minutes, add mirin, scallions, and Chinese cabbage, and cook 5 minutes more.

Add the mochi to the soup when the cabbage is just tender, and simmer very briefly while dissolving the miso in a little of the broth. Add the miso, remove from heat, and let rest for 1-2 minutes before serving.

Chapter Two:
Basics and Side Dishes

STEAMED WHITE AROMATIC RICE

8 servings

White or partially milled aromatic rices, whether basmati, Texmati, or other light varieties, go well with curries and spicy dishes of all kinds.

2 cups white aromatic rice
4 cups water

Note: Use 1 cup white aromatic rice to 2 cups water for every 4 people you are serving.

Check the rice for any small stones, then rinse it in several changes of water to remove dust and starch. Drain in a fine-mesh strainer. Place drained rice and measured water into a pot, and let it soak for 30 minutes.

Bring to a boil, then reduce to a simmer, cover tightly, and cook for 15 minutes or until the surface of the rice is pocked with little holes and most of the water is absorbed. Turn heat to very low and steam for 10-15 minutes more or until all the water is absorbed. Fluff into a serving bowl.

WILD RICE

Properly cooked wild rice increases in volume about four times. One cup uncooked yields about 4 cups cooked.

1 cup wild rice
4 cups water

Thoroughly rinse the rice in several changes of water, then drain in a fine-mesh strainer. Place the rice and measured water in a pot and bring to a boil. Lower the heat, cover, and cook for about 50 minutes, or until the rice splits and fluffs up. Drain off excess cooking water.

Note: To cut cooking time, or to cook with brown rice, soak well-rinsed wild rice in water to cover overnight or all day. Drain off soaking water, and measure fresh water to cook.

WILD RICE WITH QUINOA

Serves 2-4

A fluffy, light, disarmingly simple dish of complementary flavors and textures. Serve it, instead of potatoes, with a gravy or sauce. To cook the grains to perfection, set a timer and add the quinoa at precisely the right moment.

2½ cups water
1 teaspoon natural soy sauce
½ cup wild rice, soaked, rinsed, and drained
½ cup quinoa

Combine the water and soy sauce in a pot and bring to a boil over medium-high heat. Add the wild rice, cover, reduce heat, and simmer for 30 minutes. Add the quinoa, cover, and simmer for 20 minutes or until the water is absorbed. Remove from heat and allow to steam, covered, for 5 minutes. Fluff with a fork.

BROWN RICE WITH WHEATBERRIES
AND CHIVES

Serves 6-8

½ cup whole wheat berries
1½ cups brown rice
3 cups water
sea salt
⅓ cup minced chives

Rinse wheat berries and soak in water to cover overnight or all day. Drain.

Rinse rice, drain, and combine with the wheat, water, and a pinch of salt in a four-quart pressure cooker. Afix lid. Bring to full pressure over high heat, then lower heat and place a flame tamer under the pot. Cook for 50-60 minutes and remove from heat. When the pressure has come down, remove the cover and fluff the grain with a wooden spoon. Gently mix in the chives, cover loosely, and let rest for a few minutes before serving.

Note: If you are not using a pressure cooker, bring wheat berries and soaking water to a boil, then remove from heat and let soak, covered, for several hours or overnight. Drain, and combine the wheat with the rice, salt, and 3½ cups of water. Cover, and bring to a boil. Reduce heat and simmer for 50-60 minutes, or until the wheat berries are tender. Fluff the grain and mix in the chives as above.

WALNUT RICE

Serves 6-8

¾ cup shelled walnuts
2 cups long grain brown rice
½ teaspoon sea salt
4 cups water
⅓ cup minced parsley

Preheat oven to 350°F and roast the walnuts on a baking sheet for 15-20 minutes or just until golden and fragrant. Rinse rice, drain, and combine all ingredients except parsley in a pot. Cover and bring to a boil, then lower the heat and simmer for 45 minutes or until the rice is tender. (If the top of the rice looks dry, mix it under and cook over very low heat for 5-10 more minutes.) Remove from the heat and fluff gently while mixing in the parsley.

RICE WITH BARLEY AND WATERCRESS

Serves 4-6

Combinations for grain-vegetable side dishes are endless. This one is lovely with fish.

1½ cups short grain brown rice
½ cup barley
3 cups water
sea salt
½ cup watercress, chopped into ½-inch lengths

Rinse rice and barley and drain. Place grains, water, and a pinch of salt in a four-quart pressure cooker, and afix lid. Bring up to pressure over high heat. Lower heat and place a flame tamer under the pot. Cook for 50 minutes, then remove from heat and allow the pressure to come down. Uncover, and gently mix in the watercress.

RISI BISI

Serves 4-6

Rice is a favorite grain in Italy. Our version of risi bisi, a refreshing, traditional side dish from Venice, is made with brown rather than the usual white rice.

2 cups cooked long or medium grain brown rice
1 cup fresh peas, shucked, or frozen peas, thawed
1-2 tablespoons lemon juice
1 tablespoon extra virgin olive oil
1 teaspoon sea salt

Steam or blanch the peas just until they are tender but still firm and bright green. Mix cooked rice, lemon juice, oil, and salt together. Add drained peas, toss gently, and serve, garnished with slices of lemon, at room temperature.

STIR-FRIED RICE WITH MUSTARD GREENS

Serves 4-6

A simple stir-fry, pungent and good. Turnip greens work well, too.

1 bunch mustard greens
¼ cup toasted sesame seeds
1½ tablespoons extra virgin olive oil
4-5 cups any cooked rice (except sweet brown)
2 or more cloves garlic (to taste), minced
½ teaspoon sea salt

Wash the greens very well. Lay leaves out flat, stacked atop each other. Roll up into a bundle and slice crosswise thinly. Toast seeds in a dry pan over medium-low heat, stirring constantly just until they begin to pop and are fragrant.

Heat the oil in a skillet over medium flame and add the rice, garlic, and salt. When the rice is heated through, add the greens, mix gently, and cook for about 3 more minutes, just until greens are tender but still bright green. Turn out into serving bowl and sprinkle with sesame seeds.

BROILED MOCHI WITH SWEET
MISO TOPPING

This delicious side dish or snack goes together in no time.

¼ cup mellow white miso
1 tablespoon lemon juice
2 tablespoons rice syrup
1 tablespoon mirin
1 tablespoon tahini
1 teaspoon juice squeezed from grated fresh ginger
2 tablespoons water
12 pieces mochi, each about 2 inches x 3 inches

To make topping, combine the first 7 ingredients in a suribachi or mash together in a small bowl.

Place mochi pieces on an oiled baking sheet or broiling pan. Broil on both sides just until skin is crisp and golden and mochi is slightly puffed. (Watch carefully to prevent overcooking, in which the mochi can burst and melt completely.) Spread a thin layer of topping on each piece and broil for one minute more, or just until the topping is lightly browned.

PAN-FRIED MOCHI WITH
GINGER-SHOYU DIP

Serves 2

This recipe is pure traditional Japanese—simple, nutritious, and flavorful.

light sesame oil
6 pieces mochi, 2 inches x 2½ inches each
⅔ cup water
2-inch piece kombu
1 tablespoon natural soy sauce
2 teaspoons mirin
1 teaspoon finely grated peeled fresh ginger
3 tablespoons finely grated daikon (optional)

Place a large skillet over medium heat and brush with oil. Add mochi pieces, keeping space between them, and cook, covered, for 5 minutes or until slightly browned. Flip, cover, and cook for a few minutes more. Watch carefully so mochi doesn't overcook and melt.

To make dip sauce, bring water and kombu to a simmer in a small saucepan, then remove kombu. Add shoyu and mirin, simmer for 1 minute, and remove from heat. Add ginger and, if using, daikon. Serve 3 pieces of mochi surrounding a small bowlful of dip sauce on each plate.

PUM BUK
(Sweet Brown Rice with Aduki Beans and Winter Squash)

Serves 4-6

This simple, hearty side dish highlights the rich sweetness of the vegetable kingdom. It is a mainstay of the traditional Korean New Year's celebration. Serve it with a crisp vegetable stir-fry.

½ cup dried shelled chestnuts
½ cup aduki beans
1 cup sweet brown rice
3 cups cubed peeled butternut squash
2½ cups water
½ teaspoon sea salt

Soak chestnuts and beans, separately, in water to cover for a minimum of six hours, or bring 2 two-quart pots of water to a boil and add the chestnuts and beans separately to hot water, allowing them to soak for 2 hours. Place all ingredients in a pressure cooker, bring to pressure, turn down heat, and cook for 50 minutes. (For pot-boiling, use 3 cups water and cover tightly.) Turn out into a colorful serving bowl and garnish with chopped scallions, chives, or parsley.

Chapter Three:
One-Dish Meals

STIR-FRIED BASMATI RICE
AND ASPARAGUS

Serves 4

Whether you use brown basmati or white, cook this dish in a cast iron skillet for best results. In summer, place the skillet on a grate over an outdoor wood fire and taste the delicious difference.

4 tablespoons light sesame oil
1 small onion, cut in half then sliced thin
1 teaspoon sea salt
½ pound asparagus, cut into l-inch pieces (or broccoli, florets broken
  into l-inch pieces, stems peeled and sliced thin on the diagonal)
1 tablespoon brown rice vinegar
1½ cups cooked basmati rice

Heat the oil in a skillet, add the onion and salt, and sauté for 5 minutes, until the onions are just soft. Add the asparagus and sauté for a minute more. Add the vinegar and the rice, and sauté until the rice is heated through.

ARBORIO WITH GREEN PEAS AND CHIVES

Serves 4-6

Arborio is an Italian white rice, partially polished but still containing the germ. It is getting easier to find as it becomes more popular. Look for it in specialty food shops and the gourmet section of supermarkets. This treatment is classic Italian—refreshing and satisfying—and proves the natural affinity of rice and peas.

3 cups cooked arborio (see below)
romaine lettuce
¼ cup fresh peas, shucked
2 tablespoons finely chopped fresh chives
½ teaspoon finely chopped fresh hot pepper, seeds and veins
   removed—wear rubber gloves (optional)
1 tablespoon chopped Italian parsley
2 tablespoons extra virgin olive oil
2 tablespoons white wine vinegar or cider vinegar
1 tablespoon Dijon mustard
⅛ teaspoon paprika
⅛-¼ teaspoon dried oregano
¼-½ teaspoon sea salt

For 3 cups of cooked arborio use 2¼ cups dry measure. Rinse the rice with cold water, drain through a fine mesh strainer, and add it to 6-7 cups of boiling water along with 1 teaspoon of oil. Keep at a rolling boil, uncovered, for 10-15 minutes—much as you would with noodles. After 9-10 minutes check—also as you would noodles—and remove from the heat and drain as soon as the grains are al dente, not mushy. Rinse immediately with cold water, and drain well.

   Place cooled rice on a bed of romaine on a platter. Parboil peas by boiling in water to cover just until they are bright green and tender, 1-3 minutes. Rinse them with cold water immediately and sprinkle them over the rice. Sprinkle chives, pepper, and parsley over. Whisk remaining ingredients together, and pour this dressing over.

STIR-FRIED RICE WITH TEMPEH

Serves 3-4

Tempeh is a cultured soy product native to Indonesia and fast gaining popularity in the West because of its healthfulness and versatility. Its unique flavor goes well with rice and vegetables.

The secret to this simple, tasty stir-fry is speed. Have all the ingredients prepared before you heat the pan, and then work quickly. Add a handful of mung bean sprouts in the last step for "Chinese leftovers."

5-6 ounces tempeh
3 tablespoons oil
2 cloves garlic, minced
1 egg, lightly beaten
1½ cups cooked brown rice, well cooled or chilled
⅓ cup chopped scallion
2 teaspoons natural soy sauce

To prepare the tempeh, cut it into pieces each about ½ -inch by 1 inch. Soak the pieces briefly in salted water (in a bowl combine 1 teaspoon sea salt with 1 cup cool water), pat dry, and deep- or pan-fry them in any light oil until golden. Drain on paper.

Place a wok or skillet over medium heat and add the 3 tablespoons oil. Add the garlic and sauté for 15 seconds. Add the egg and scramble briefly. Add the rice and stir-fry for 2 minutes. Add the scallion, fried tempeh pieces, and the soy sauce, stir-frying until just heated through. Serve immediately.

SALMON FRIED RICE

Serves 4

Rice is an excellent foil to many seafoods. Peas turn up here, too, in a dish that is quick, elegant, and tasty.

½ pound salmon fillets
2 tablespoons mirin
2 tablespoons any light oil for pan-frying
1 teaspoon peeled and grated fresh ginger
1 onion, minced
3 ribs celery and leaves, chopped
4 cups cooked rice, any kind except sweet brown
2 tablespoons natural soy sauce
1 cup green peas, shucked fresh, or frozen
1 tablespoon sake or dry white wine

Broil the salmon brushed with the mirin for 10-12 minutes or just until it flakes easily. Separate into bite-size pieces.

Heat a wok or large skillet and add the oil and ginger. Add onion, and sauté briefly over medium-high heat. Add celery, and continue to sauté for 3-5 minutes, or until celery is almost tender. Add rice and soy sauce, stir once, cover, and cook for 5 minutes. Add peas, salmon, and sake, and cook for 2-3 more minutes, covered, or just until the peas are tender but still bright green and the salmon is heated through.

RICE PILAF

Serves 4

Flavorful and nutritious rice pilaf is an excellent way to introduce someone to brown rice. The soy sauce-seasoned vegetable stock in this version is a good foundation for many dishes—other grains, soups, stews, and sauces.

3 cups vegetable stock (see below)
1-1½ tablespoons olive oil
1 large clove garlic, minced
1 medium onion, diced
1 rib celery, diced
6 mushrooms, chopped
pinch sea salt
1½ cups medium grain brown rice, washed and drained
1 bay leaf
1 tablespoon natural soy sauce
¼ cup minced parsley
½ cup toasted chopped almonds

To prepare stock, in a saucepan combine 4-5 cups water; 1 onion with skin, quartered; 1 rib celery, chopped; several sprigs parsley; a 6-inch strip of kombu (optional); 1 bay leaf; and a sprig of fresh or pinch of dried rosemary or thyme. Bring to a boil, reduce heat, and simmer for 15-20 minutes. Strain, set aside bay leaf, and discard solids.

Toast almonds on a baking sheet in a preheated 350°F oven until just fragrant and golden, about 10-15 minutes. Let cool, and chop.

In a pot over medium heat sauté the garlic and onion in the olive oil until the onion is translucent, about 5 minutes. Add the celery, mushrooms, and salt, and sauté for 2-3 minutes more. Add the rice and stir. Add 3 cups of hot stock, the bay leaf, and the soy sauce. Bring to a boil, cover, lower heat, and simmer for 50 minutes or until all liquid is absorbed. Remove from heat and discard bay leaf. Mix in the almonds and parsley (reserve a little of both for garnish), cover, and let rest for 5-10 minutes.

Garnish with reserved chopped almonds and parsley.

WILD RICE PILAF

Makes 6½ cups

Stuff a rich, sweet squash, such as buttercup or hokkaido pumpkin, with wild rice pilaf for a special Thanksgiving dinner.

¼ cup pine nuts
1 tablespoon light sesame oil
4 shallots, sliced thin
3 cups water
1¾ cups brown aromatic rice
¼ cup wild rice (for preparation, see page 22)
½ cup grated carrot
2 tablespoons natural soy sauce
2 teaspoons dried thyme
1 teaspoon dried marjoram
½ cup finely chopped parsley

In a preheated 350°F oven toast the pine nuts on a baking sheet for 3-5 minutes or just until they are barely golden. Heat the oil in a three-quart saucepan over medium heat and sauté the shallots until they are tender, about 5 minutes. Bring the water to a boil in another pot. Rinse and drain the rices, add to the shallots, and stir well. When the water boils, add it to the rice along with the carrot, soy sauce, thyme, and marjoram. When boiling resumes, turn heat to low, cover, and simmer for 1 hour. Place a flame tamer under the pot for the last 30 minutes.

To serve, alternate layers of rice mixture with the parsley and pine nuts in a large bowl and then toss gently.

TWO RICES WITH HERBS

Serves 6

This is a wonderful Thanksgiving side dish.

½ cup wild rice
2½ cups long grain brown rice
½ cup toasted pumpkin seeds
2 tablespoons light sesame oil
½ teaspoon each dried rosemary and sage
½-1 teaspoon sea salt, to taste
5 cups water
2 teaspoons fresh thyme leaves (optional)
3 tablespoons chopped fresh parsley
1 teaspoon umeboshi vinegar

Rinse wild rice very well, and soak in water to cover for several hours or overnight. Drain. Rinse brown rice and drain. Toast pumpkin seeds in a dry skillet over medium heat, stirring constantly, for 5-10 minutes or until they are golden and fragrant and begin to pop.

Place a pot over medium heat and add the oil. Add rosemary, sage, salt, and both rices, and sauté for 3-5 minutes, stirring constantly. Add the water and bring to a boil. Turn heat to low, add thyme if using, cover, and let cook for 50-60 minutes, or until water is absorbed and rice is tender.

Gently mix in the remaining ingredients, and fluff into a brightly colored bowl to serve.

RICE, RADISHES, AND WALNUTS WITH BASIL PESTO

Serves 4-6

This simple, flavorful dish with the crunch of radishes goes well with broiled fish.

1 cup chopped toasted walnuts
3 cups cooked rice, white or brown
1 cup chopped fresh basil
1 tablespoon minced garlic
¼ cup lemon juice
¼ cup extra virgin olive oil
1 teaspoon sea salt
1 tablespoon white wine vinegar
½ cup red radishes, cut in half and sliced into thin half-moons

Before chopping, toast walnuts on a baking sheet in a preheated 350°F oven for 10-15 minutes or just until golden and fragrant.

Combine rice and walnuts in a bowl. Place basil, garlic, lemon juice, oil, salt, and vinegar into a blender and process until well mixed. Mix into the rice and walnuts along with the radishes, reserving a few radish slices to arrange on top as a garnish. This is good with warm, freshly cooked rice as well as with leftover cooled rice.

MUJADDARAH
(Middle Eastern Rice and Lentils)

Serves 6

This delicious Middle Eastern dish is often called "the meat of the poor." It is traditionally served with Syrian bread and a yogurt dish.

2 cups brown (green) lentils
½ cup long grain brown rice
olive oil for sautéeing
1 large onion, diced
sea salt to taste
½ teaspoon each cinnamon and allspice
4¼ cups water
2 large Spanish or red onions, sliced

Rinse the lentils and drain. Rinse the rice and drain.

Heat 2 tablespoons of oil in an 8-quart saucepan and add the diced onion along with a generous pinch of salt and the spices. Sauté over medium heat, stirring often, just until the onions are translucent. Add lentils and rice to the pot, and stir and sauté for a few minutes more. Add the water and bring to a boil. Cover, reduce heat to low, and simmer for 45-60 minutes or until all the water is absorbed and the mixture is tender and slightly dry. Transfer to a large platter.

While the lentils are cooking, slice the 2 Spanish or red onions into crescents, and sauté them in the remaining oil in a skillet, stirring often, until they are very dark brown but not scorched. Cover the mujaddarah with a blanket of the piping hot onions and serve immediately.

DAL AND RICE CASSEROLE WITH SPICED ONIONS

Serves 4-6

In India, dals are thick bean soups with heavenly combinations of spices. Here we use the theme to give everyday rice-and-beans a delicious twist. For a luncheon loaf, bake the dish in a glass bread pan and let it cool to room temperature before slicing.

DAL AND RICE CASSEROLE

1 tablespoon extra virgin olive oil
2 cups diced onions
1½ teaspoons sea salt
¼ teaspoon each cardamom powder and turmeric
½ teaspoon cumin powder
¾ cup red lentils, rinsed and drained
¾ cup brown rice, rinsed and drained
3 cups water or stock
oil and cornmeal for pan

Preheat oven to 400°F. Oil casserole or loaf pan and dust with cornmeal.

Place a pot over medium heat and add the olive oil. Add the onions and sauté until translucent, 3-5 minutes. Add the salt and spices and cook, stirring, for 2 more minutes. Add lentils, rice, and water and bring to a boil. Reduce heat to simmer, and cook for 15 minutes. Remove from heat and pour into prepared baking dish. Cover tightly and bake for 30 minutes at 400°F, then reduce temperature to 350°F, uncover, and bake for another 35 minutes. Remove from oven and allow to rest for 20 minutes before serving with Spiced Onions.

SPICED ONIONS

1 tablespoon extra virgin olive oil
1½ cups onions, cut into half-moon slivers
1 teaspoon sea salt
¼ teaspoon cardamom powder
¼ teaspoon cumin powder
2 tablespoons lemon juice

Place a skillet over medium heat and add the oil. Add onions and salt and turn heat to low. Add cardamom and cumin, and cook slowly until the onions are limp, about 10 minutes. Add lemon juice, turn heat to medium-high, and cook for 2 minutes, stirring constantly. Remove from heat, and top each serving of casserole or loaf with 1 tablespoonful.

RICE BIRYANI

Serves 6-8

Biryani, Indian pilaf, is a meal in itself. A unique blend of grains, herbs, vegetables, spices, nuts, and dried fruits, it is one of India's most colorful creations.

2 cups white basmati rice
1 tablespoon light sesame oil
1 Spanish onion
2-3 cloves garlic, crushed or minced
¼ cup cashews or cashew pieces
½ teaspoon curry powder
1½ cinnamon sticks
6 whole green cardamoms
6 whole cloves
4 bay leaves
¼ cup seedless raisins
1 cup fresh corn kernels
1 cup sliced green beans
1 cup diced carrots
1 cup fresh peas
¼ teaspoon cayenne powder
4 cups water
1 teaspoon sea salt
fresh cilantro for garnish

Wash and drain the rice. Break off the round ends of the cloves and discard.

Heat the oil over medium-low in a heavy pot. Add the onion and sauté until golden, about 10 minutes. Add the garlic and cashews and stir. Add the curry powder, cinnamon, cardamoms, clove stems, and bay leaves, and stir. Add the raisins and remaining vegetables, and stir again. Add the cayenne, if using, and the rice. Stir, add the water and salt, and bring to a boil. Cover, reduce heat, and simmer for 20 minutes or just until rice and vegetables are tender. Remove bay leaves and serve garnished with chopped cilantro.

JAMBALAYA

Serves 5-6

The popular south Louisiana Cajun dish, with the distinctive flavor of thyme. You can substitute other shellfish, or any firm-fleshed white fish, for the shrimp.

1 tablespoon hot pepper oil
1 tablespoon whole wheat flour
1 medium yellow onion, diced (¾-1 cup)
1 clove garlic, minced
2¼ cups fresh ripe or canned tomatoes, diced
1 bay leaf
2 tablespoons fresh or ½ tablespoon dried thyme
¾ teaspoon sea salt
1½ cup water or stock
1 cup long grain white or brown rice, washed and drained
1 cup diced green pepper
½ cup chopped parsley
1 cup chopped celery (about 3 stalks)
2 scallions, sliced thin
½ pound small or medium shrimp, shelled and deveined
freshly ground black pepper, to taste

Heat the oil in a heavy saucepan. Add the flour and stir constantly over medium heat until fragrant, about 3 minutes. Add onion, garlic, tomatoes, bay leaf, thyme, and salt, and stir. Reduce heat, cover, and let simmer for 10 minutes. Remove from heat and add 1½ cups water or stock to the mixture. Return to pot and add rice, green pepper, parsley, celery, and scallion. Cover, and cook over medium-low heat for 15 minutes. Add shrimp, cover, and cook for 3-5 minutes more. Remove from heat and let stand, covered, for 10 minutes. Remove bay leaf. Add pepper and serve, accompanied by crusty French bread.

SHRIMP BIRYANI

Serves 6

This biryani is festively colored with aromatic saffron—a costly ingredient, but well worth it in heavenly aroma and flavor for a special occasion. In India this biryani is served at weddings, the boiled egg garnish symbolizing fertility and prosperity.

You will need a heavy, ovenproof pot of at least six-quart capacity with a tight-fitting lid. Enameled cast iron is good, as is heat-resistant glassware such as Pyrex, or a covered casserole.

2 pounds medium or large shrimp
2 large onions
2-inch piece fresh ginger, peeled and sliced (2 tablespoons)
6 cloves garlic, peeled and sliced
¼ cup lemon juice
3 tablespoons ghee or light oil
1 tablespoon each: whole cloves, black peppercorns, fennel seeds, black
*   mustard seeds, coriander seeds, and cumin seeds, ground coarsely*
*   in a spice or coffee mill*
2 teaspoons sea salt
1 cup yogurt
1½ cups aromatic rice
½ cup cow's milk or plain soymilk
½ teaspoon saffron (½ gram compressed before measuring)
½ cup golden raisins
1 cup toasted cashews
1 hard-boiled egg, sliced thin, for garnish (optional)

Peel, devein, and rinse shrimp. Set aside. Quarter one onion and place in a food processor or blender. Add ginger and garlic to the processor, and purée. Add lemon juice, pulse a few times, and pour mixture into a bowl. Thinly slice the other onion. Heat ghee or oil in a heavy skillet, add sliced onion, spices, and salt, and sauté over medium heat for about 10 minutes, until onions are tender. Remove from heat and stir in the yogurt. Add to mixture in bowl and mix together well. Cover and refrigerate until needed. (It will keep up to 2 days before cooking.)

About 2 hours before serving biryani, bring 4 cups of water to a boil. Reduce heat, add washed rice, and simmer for 10 minutes. Drain in a fine-mesh strainer. Place shrimp with marinade into the baking dish, gently pour in the rice, and smooth the top. Preheat oven to 350°F.

Make saffron milk: Heat milk to simmer with saffron threads. Remove from heat and let steep for 2 minutes. Pour carefully, in streaks, over the rice, and distribute the raisins evenly over the top. Cover the dish and bake for 35 minutes.

Toast cashews on a baking sheet in a preheated 350°F oven for 5-10 minutes or just until golden and fragrant.

To serve—in the pot or transferred to a bowl—decorate with egg rounds and cashews.

SAYYADIYYEH
(Middle Eastern Fish and Rice with Taratour Sauce)

Serves 6-8

This wonderful, golden yellow rice dish is popular in coastal towns bordering the Mediterranean Sea—each has its own variation. Almost any fish is suitable, as long as it is thick and firm enough to be broken into chunks. One variation calls for simmering the head of the fish in water to make a rich stock in which to boil the rice. Traditionally the fish is fried, but it's just as good broiled. Serve with taratour (recipe follows) and a crisp green salad.

2 pounds fish (haddock, cod, halibut, or pollock), whole or fillets
2 cups uncooked aromatic or brown rice
light sesame or olive oil for sautéing
2 large onions, chopped
3 cups water
1-2 teaspoons sea salt
1 teaspoon turmeric

MARINADE

½ cup lemon juice
4 tablespoons olive oil
2 cloves garlic, crushed
1 teaspoon sea salt

Combine marinade ingredients and allow fish to soak in it for at least 10 minutes. Sauté the onions in a little oil until they are golden brown, about 10 minutes. In a large pot combine the rice, sautéed onions, water, salt, and turmeric. Bring to a boil, reduce to lowest possible heat, and simmer for 50-60 minutes or until all the water is absorbed.

Broil the fish (with all its marinade) on both sides until lightly browned. Add any extra "sauce" to the taratour.

Cut fish into chunks and debone. Heap the rice onto a platter, place fish on top, and pour taratour over all.

TARATOUR SAUCE

Makes ¾ cup

Most seafood dishes in the Middle East are served with taratour—and it is a delicious touch.

1 clove garlic, crushed
¼ cup lemon juice
pinch sea salt
6 tablespoons tahini
water for thinning (about 2 tablespoons)
3-4 sprigs parsley, chopped fine

Combine the garlic, lemon juice, and salt in a small bowl. Slowly add the tahini, stirring constantly. Add the parsley. Add water gradually, stirring, until a pancake-batter consistency is reached.

Spoon taratour onto individual servings of sayyadiyyeh.

RICE AND PISTACHIO NUT BURGERS

Makes six 3-inch burgers

This is a good way to use leftover cooked rice.

It calls for a handful each of toasted pistachios and pumpkin seeds, but you can substitute sesame seeds or other nuts you have on hand.

Toast and lightly grind sesame seeds, and toast and chop nuts (see below).

A roasted sweet pepper, green or red, can fill out the flavor of any dish when it needs a little something extra. Once you get used to the procedure, it is not at all daunting. Skewer a pepper on a fork and hold it close to a medium-low flame on the stove until the skin is well scorched, turning it to blacken evenly all around. Put the piping hot pepper into a heavy bowl and cover tightly. Let it steam for 10-15 minutes, when the skin will slip off when you scrape it lightly. Remove all the skin, and the seeds and stem, and chop.

⅛ cup pistachio nuts, toasted and chopped coarsely
⅛ cup pumpkin seeds, toasted and chopped coarsely
2½ cups cooked rice
3 level tablespoons mellow miso
⅓ cup finely minced scallion
⅓ cup finely minced parsley
1 sweet pepper, roasted and diced
approximately ¼ cup whole wheat or unbleached white flour
2-3 tablespoons any light oil for pan-frying

To toast nuts and pumpkin seeds, spread them on a dry baking sheet and roast them in a 350°F preheated oven for 10-15 minutes or until just fragrant and golden. (Toast sesame seeds in a dry pan over medium-low heat, stirring constantly just until they begin to pop and are fragrant.)

In a mixing bowl cut the miso into the rice with the side of a rice paddle or a wooden spoon. Add the scallion, parsley, pepper, and seeds and nuts. Mix in the flour a little at time until the mixture is fairly dry, not too sticky, and holds its shape well. Moisten your hands with a little water or vegetable oil and shape burgers. If they are sticky, lightly dust both sides with flour before cooking.

Heat the oil in a large skillet over medium-low, add the burgers, cover the pan, reduce heat to low, and cook 10-15 minutes until golden brown.

Flip, and cook the other side. Sprinkle with natural soy sauce, or melt a slice of cheese on top after you have flipped them. Serve as you would any burger, with pickles and trimmings, or as a croquette, with gravy or sauce.

OPEN-FACE VEGETABLE BURGER WITH MUSHROOM GRAVY

Serves 4-6

BURGER

½ cup toasted sunflower seeds
1½ cups cooked chick peas, lentils, or aduki beans
1 cup cooked rice
½ cup grated carrot
1 cup diced onion
1 cup diced green pepper
¼ cup chopped parsley
1 tablespoon chopped fresh thyme, or 1 teaspoon dried
2 tablespoons natural soy sauce
⅓ cup whole wheat pastry flour, or corn flour
¼ cup cornmeal to coat burgers
oil for pan-frying

MUSHROOM GRAVY

2 cups water
1½ cups chopped mushrooms
½ cup diced onion
1 tablespoon caraway seeds
3 tablespoons natural soy sauce
2½ tablespoons arrowroot powder dissolved in ½ cup cool water

Toast seeds on a baking sheet in a preheated 350°F oven for 10-15 minutes or just until golden and fragrant.

Mash the beans. Mix first nine ingredients together, and bind with the pastry or corn flour. Form into burgers, coat lightly with cornmeal, and pan-fry until golden on both sides, turning once. Drain on paper.

To make the gravy, bring the 2 cups of water to a boil and add the mushrooms and onion. Reduce to a simmer, and cook for 5 minutes or until the onions are transparent and the mushrooms are soft. Add caraway seeds and soy sauce. Add diluted arrowroot and cook, stirring constantly, just until the gravy is transparent and has thickened, about 3-5 minutes.

Serve as an open-face sandwich, accompanied by lettuce, tomato, and dill pickles, or as croquettes with sauce.

RICE CROQUETTES

Makes eight 3-inch patties

½-1 cup ground toasted almonds, or 1 pound white fish fillet (steamed
  until just tender) and ½ teaspoon peeled and grated ginger root
3 cups cooked short-grain brown rice
2 medium onions, minced
1 rib celery, minced
½ teaspoon sea salt or 2 tablespoons natural soy sauce, to taste
¼ cup whole wheat flour, more or less as necessary
¼ cup safflower oil
2 scallions, slivered, for garnish

Toast almonds on a baking sheet in a preheated 350°F oven for 10-15 minutes or just until golden and fragrant. Let cool completely before grinding in a blender or coffee mill.

Combine the rice, vegetables, almonds (or fish and ginger), and seasoning. Add flour a very little at a time, as necessary to obtain a consistency that holds together well (you may not need any). Form patties, using moistened hands if necessary, dust with flour, and pan-fry in heated oil over moderate heat for 10 minutes on each side, or until golden brown and crispy. Garnish with the scallions to serve.

Variations are as many as your larder and imagination can come up with: substitute other cooked grains, add herbs or spices, use up leftover cooked beans, use bread crumbs or cornmeal for a crunchy coating, or serve with a clear vegetable sauce or gravy.

GARDEN PAELLA WITH SHRIMP
AND MUSSELS

Serves 4-6

This version of a traditional Spanish dish skips the usual chicken and chorizo sausage, but the mainstay ingredients of rice, olive oil, and saffron are complemented nicely by fish and vegetables.

2 quarts boiling water
2 tablespoons extra virgin olive oil
2 cups diced onion
3 tablespoons minced garlic
1 cup sliced celery
1 cup shelled peas, fresh or frozen
1½ teaspoons sea salt
1 teaspoon Herbamare
2 teaspoons crushed saffron
2 cups short grain brown rice
2 cups chopped tomatoes (approximately 4 tomatoes)
2 roasted green peppers, peeled, seeded, and diced
2 roasted red peppers, peeled, seeded, and diced
1 pound medium shrimp, peeled and deveined
½ cup and 3 tablespoons white wine
1 pound mussels, farmed or cultured (if available)
2 scallions, sliced thin
¼ cup green olives, pitted and sliced in half
¼ cup black olives, pitted and sliced in half

In a four-quart pot, sauté the olive oil, onions, and garlic over medium heat. Cook for about 5 minutes or until the onions are translucent. Add the celery, green peas, salt, Herbamare, and saffron, and cook for another 2 minutes. Add the rice and 4 cups of boiling water. Bring to a boil, turn down to a simmer, and put over flame tamer. Cook for 50 minutes.

Cut an x on the top and bottom of each tomato. Place the tomatoes in the remaining 4 cups of boiling water. Leave in the water for 1 minute, then remove the tomatoes with a slotted spoon. Peel the tomatoes (the peels should slide right off) and cut them in half. Sprinkle the cut side of each tomato with sea salt, place them with the salt side down on a platter, and let them sit for 20 minutes. Squeeze the seeds out of the tomatoes, chop them, and set aside.

When the rice has cooked for 50 minutes add the tomatoes, roasted peppers, shrimp, and 3 tablespoons of wine. Cook 5 more minutes or until the shrimp is pink.

Rinse the mussels and pull off the "hairy beard." Place the mussels in a pot with ½ cup of wine and bring to a boil. Turn down slightly and cook for 6 minutes, or up to 10 minutes if the mussels are very large. Discard any mussels that remain closed after cooking.

Serve the paella on a platter surrounded by mussels, and garnish the rice with the olives and scallions.

Chapter Four: Rice and...

MEDIUM GRAIN BROWN RICE WITH SCALLION-MISO SAUCE

Makes 4 servings

Medium grain brown rice is closer to short grain than to long grain in appearance and taste. It is delicious either pressure cooked or boiled, but, as with all the brown rices, it is richer and more flavorful with pressure cooking.

You can combine the dark sesame oil half and half with light (unroasted) sesame oil for a milder taste.

1 bunch scallions (¼ pound or about 2 cups cut)
2 tablespoons dark sesame oil
1 tablespoon barley miso
4 cups freshly cooked medium grain brown rice

Wash scallions, trim off roots and ends, and cut into ½ -inch pieces, keeping the white parts separate from the green. Heat the oil in a two-quart pot and sauté the white scallion parts over medium heat for 2 minutes. Add green parts, reduce heat, cover, and cook for 2-4 minutes or until almost tender. Arrange miso by little dabs on top of the scallions, cover the pot, and cook for 2 minutes more. Stir, and serve. Figure on about 2 tablespoons of sauce per one-cup serving of rice.

RICE AND MILLET WITH SPICY PEANUT SAUCE

Serves 6-8

A taste of the Orient, with a humble name and wonderful flavor. The unusual—and hot—peanut sauce is made hearty and rich by cooking. Serve it over any brown rice to enliven a simple winter meal.

1 cup medium grain brown rice
1 cup millet
3½ cups water
½-1 teaspoon sea salt, to taste

Wash the grains, drain them well, and toast them, stirring constantly, in a skillet or stainless steel pan over medium-low heat until dry and fragrant, about 15 minutes. Add water and salt, and bring to a boil. Reduce heat and simmer, covered, for 50-60 minutes. Fluff with a fork.

SPICY PEANUT SAUCE

Makes 2½ cups

1 tablespoon dark sesame oil, or ½ tablespoon each dark and light
1 small onion, diced
1 tablespoon minced garlic
1½ teaspoons bottled hot pepper sauce
¼ cup natural soy sauce
1 teaspoon cumin powder
¼-1 teaspoon cayenne powder, to taste
1 teaspoon Chinese 5-spice powder
1 cup peanut butter
3 tablespoons maple syrup
2 tablespoons lemon juice
1 cup water
1 cup chopped chives, parsley, or cilantro

Place a small skillet over medium heat and add the oil. Add onion and garlic, and sauté until the onion is translucent, 3-5 minutes. Add hot pepper sauce, soy sauce, cumin, cayenne, and 5-spice, and cook for 2 minutes, stirring. Remove from heat.

In a bowl combine peanut butter, syrup, lemon juice, and water. Add the onion-spice mixture and mix well. Add the fresh herb, mix, and serve immediately over freshly cooked rice and millet. This is also good on noodles or a parboiled salad.

SWEET AND SOUR SEITAN WITH RICE

Serves 6-8

Seitan is much like beef in taste and texture, and can be used in much the same way. Deep-frying in a batter, however, is an un-beeflike preparation that proves seitan's versatility…and makes it incredibly delicious and succulent. Surrounding it with a sweet and sour sauce is positively decadent. Serve the dish with fresh rice (any kind) and a crisp green salad.

Look for seitan in the cooler section of a natural foods store.

2 cups whole wheat pastry flour
3 tablespoons arrowroot powder
¼ teaspoon sea salt

Combine all ingredients to make tempura batter and mix until smooth. If you prefer a thinner batter, add a little more water.

5 cups seitan, pressed briefly to squeeze out excess juice and cut into
*   large bite-size pieces*
4-6 cups oil for deep-frying (safflower works well)

Have oil very hot but not smoking. Dip seitan pieces in tempura batter and deep-fry, a few at a time, until golden. Drain on paper and set aside.

2½ cups water
⅓-½ cup natural soy sauce
4 carrots, cut in half lengthwise, then sliced thin diagonally
6 ribs celery, sliced thin diagonally

Combine water and soy sauce. Place carrots and celery in a soup pot and cover three-quarters with water-soy sauce. Bring to a boil, reduce heat, and simmer, covered, for 5-10 minutes, or until vegetables are just tender.

2 tablespoons arrowroot powder dissolved in 1 cup water
1 cup stock or water
½ cup brown rice vinegar or cider vinegar
½-¾ cup barley malt syrup
½-1 teaspoon peeled and grated fresh ginger
2 scallions, chopped

Combine all ingredients except scallions and mix well. Add to cooked vegetables, bring to simmer, and cook, stirring, until sauce is thick and clear, 3-5 minutes. Add tempura seitan, transfer to a serving bowl, and garnish with scallions.

CURRY RICE

Serves 3

This recipe looks complicated, but it goes together fast when all is prepared and at hand. Much of the preparation can be done ahead of time, and the extra steps to make it are well worth the effort.

The deep-fried tofu here is a perfect addition, since tofu has the congenial quality of absorbing surrounding flavors and surrendering them sensuously to the palate.

4 cups kombu or kombu-shiitake stock (see below)
1 pound firm tofu
2-3 cups safflower or other light oil for deep-frying tofu
1 teaspoon light sesame oil for sautéing vegetables
1 clove garlic, finely minced
1 large onion, chopped, or 1 leek, sliced on the diagonal
2 carrots, cut into chunks
1 rib celery, sliced
1 teaspoon sea salt
2-3 teaspoons curry powder, to taste
1 teaspoon cumin powder
1 tablespoon juice squeezed from peeled and grated fresh ginger
½ bay leaf
2½ cups bite-size broccoli florets
3 tablespoons mellow white miso
3 tablespoons kuzu (crush lumps before measuring)
6 cups cooked brown rice, any kind except sweet brown
chopped cilantro to garnish

To make kombu-shiitake stock, soak 3 dried shiitake mushrooms and a 6-inch piece of kombu in 4 cups of water for 15 minutes, then bring to a simmer in a pan. Remove kombu and reserve for another use. Simmer shiitake for 5 minutes, then turn off heat and allow to steep.

Cut tofu block crosswise into four or five ¾ -inch slices, then each slice diagonally into two triangular pieces. Line a baking sheet or cutting board with a clean, dry, absorbent towel, and lay tofu slices on. Fold the end of the towel over the tofu, and cover with another baking sheet. Put a weight such as a large cast iron skillet on top. Prop one end of the bottom baking sheet up an inch or so, and allow tofu to drain while you prepare the vegetables and cook the rice.

Properly fried, tofu should be crisp and golden on the outside and soft and tender, with a spongy texture, inside. The oil should be very hot (375°F) but not smoking before you slip in any pieces. Fry until golden on one side, then turn and fry until golden on the other (about 3 minutes total). Remove all pieces from one batch and place on a wire rack or absorbent paper before adding more tofu to the oil. Cut each slice of fried tofu in half again to make more triangles. Set aside.

Heat the sesame oil in a large skillet, and sauté garlic and onion or leek over medium heat for 2-3 minutes. Remove mushrooms from stock and cut off and discard stems. Slice caps and add to the skillet. Add carrots and celery and sauté for 2-3 minutes more. Add salt, curry, and cumin, and sauté briefly. Add ginger juice, 2 cups stock, bay leaf, and tofu. Cover, and simmer for 15 minutes. Add another cup of stock, bring to a simmer, add broccoli, cover, and cook for 3-5 minutes, or until broccoli is just tender-crisp. Thin the miso in 3 tablespoons water and add it to the pot along with the last cup of stock. Thoroughly dissolve the kuzu in 3 tablespoons water and add to the pot while stirring. Continue to stir gently as the sauce thickens. Simmer 1 minute more. Remove bay leaf.

To serve, spoon hot sauce over fresh rice in individual bowls. Garnish with chopped fresh cilantro.

SEITAN STROGANOFF WITH
TOFU SOUR CREAM

Serves 2-3

Meat free, dairy free, and delicious, this elegant-tasting dish is easy and fast to make. Have all ingredients prepared and measured before you begin to cook, and then try to have the rice and Stroganoff done simultaneously so they can go from pan to table piping hot and fresh.

2 large cloves garlic or 2 shallots, minced
3 tablespoons extra virgin olive oil
2 cups seitan, cut into thin, large bite-size pieces
8 ounces fresh mushrooms, sliced
pinch sea salt
pinch white or black pepper
pinch dried marjoram
pinch dried basil
¼ cup dry white wine
1 cup tofu sour cream (see below)
2 cups freshly cooked rice (any kind except sweet brown)—or noodles
3 heaping teaspoons minced parsley to garnish

TOFU SOUR CREAM

Makes 1 cup

1 pound fresh tofu, soft-style
juice of one lemon, 4-6 tablespoons
½-1 teaspoon sea salt
2 teaspoons mirin
2 tablespoons olive oil
1 tablespoon Dijon mustard
1 teaspoon umeboshi vinegar

Place tofu block in lightly salted boiling water to cover, remove pan from heat immediately, and let stand for 2-3 minutes. Drain, and cool in cold water. Place all tofu sour cream ingredients in a blender and process until smooth and the consistency of dairy sour cream. If too thick, add a little water. If too sour, add more salt.

Sauté garlic or shallots in 1 tablespoon of the oil over medium-low heat just until translucent, 1-3 minutes. Add seitan and fry for a few minutes, just until browned on both sides. Remove from pan and set aside. Add another tablespoon of oil and sauté the mushrooms with the salt for 2-3 minutes. Return seitan to pan with pepper, marjoram, and basil, and toss. Add wine and tofu sour cream and heat briefly and gently, stirring just enough to mix. Be careful not to overcook or the mixture may curdle.

To serve, warm plates, and make individual servings of fresh rice topped with Stroganoff and garnished with plenty of parsley. Steamed carrots are the perfect accompaniment.

CAJUN RED BEANS AND RICE

Serves 4-5

Every Monday all through the Louisiana bayous and up to New Orleans, it's a tradition to use the leftover ham bone from Sunday's big dinner to cook with red beans. Red beans and rice makes a delicious yet simple dish that can even be found on the menus of classy uptown restaurants as a "Monday Special." Instead of cooking the beans for 3-4 hours, as Cajun chefs do, rinse the beans and soak them all day or overnight. Also, miso or natural soy sauce here replaces the traditional seasoning of ham.

2 cups small red beans or kidney beans, rinsed and soaked
two 6-inch strips kombu
2 bay leaves
1½ cups finely chopped onion
½ teaspoon dried thyme
3 cloves garlic, minced
¾ cup minced parsley
1 cup diced green pepper
1 teaspoon sea salt
2 tablespoons red miso, mashed into ¼ cup water or stock, or natural
  soy sauce to taste
4-5 cups freshly cooked brown rice
chopped scallion for garnish

Drain the beans. Place the kombu into a pressure cooker, add beans and bay leaves and enough water (approximately 5 cups) to cover the beans, and pressure cook for 45-50 minutes. If you are not using a pressure cooker, bring the beans to a boil, turn down heat, and simmer for 1 hour, or until the beans are soft but still hold their shape.

Add onion, thyme, garlic, parsley, green pepper, and salt to pot, replace on medium-low heat, and simmer for 15-20 minutes. Add miso or soy sauce and simmer for another 5 minutes. Remove bay leaves.

For a thicker consistency, remove 1 cup of the beans, mash, and return to the pot.

To serve, place a scoop of hot rice on each plate, pour beans over, and garnish with chopped scallion.

ARROZ CON FRIJOLES COLORADOS
(Rice with Red Beans)

Serves 6-8

Rice with red beans is also a hearty Latin American one-dish meal. Any red beans, such as rositas and pintos, will do, but kidney beans are richest in color and flavor. Spice up this chili with more hot pepper, or delete it altogether for a milder dish.

1 cup red beans
3 cups water
1 three-inch piece kombu
1 tablespoon any light oil
2 ribs celery, sliced thin on the diagonal
1 carrot, cut into half moons
1 each small yellow summer squash and zucchini, cut into half moons
¼-1 teaspoon (to taste) finely chopped fresh chili pepper, seeded and deveined (wear rubber gloves)
3 cloves garlic, minced
1 cup chopped roasted red sweet pepper (see page 50)
1 tablespoon arrowroot powder or kuzu (crush before measuring)
1-2 tablespoons dark miso
1 cup chopped cilantro
freshly cooked rice, brown or white

Sort beans to remove any stones, wash, and soak them in water to cover for several hours or overnight. Drain, and combine them with water and kombu in a pot. Bring to a boil, reduce heat, cover, and simmer for 45-60 minutes or until tender. (Throughout cooking, beans should remain covered by an inch or so of water, so it may be necessary to replenish it if necessary.)

While beans cook, prepare vegetables. In a heavy saucepan or skillet, heat the oil and sauté celery, carrot, squashes, chili pepper, and garlic, adding them one at a time, cooking and stirring briefly between each addition. Sauté 2-3 minutes more, then remove from heat and cover.

When the beans are tender, strain them, reserving the liquid. Add beans to vegetables along with the roasted red pepper. Dissolve arrowroot or kuzu in ¼ cup cool water and stir into the bean liquid. Dissolve miso in a little of the liquid and add it back in. Pour bean liquid over vegetables and beans and place over medium-low heat. Cook and stir for a few minutes, until it is hot and somewhat thick. Remove from heat and stir in cilantro. Serve over fresh hot rice, accompanied by cornbread or crisp tortillas.

GINGERED TOFU AND MUSHROOMS OVER COCONUT RICE

Serves 4-6

This is a delicious import from Thailand. Lemon grass and fish sauce are integral to everyday Thai cooking and so can be found at Oriental markets and even some natural foods stores and supermarkets.

Note: Some bottled fish sauces are quite salty, so add it a little at a time, and taste to avoid over-seasoning.

2 tablespoons light or dark sesame oil, or half and half
1 medium onion, quartered and sliced thin
4 cloves garlic, minced
3 tablespoons peeled and minced fresh ginger
1 stalk lemon grass, the inner part only, sliced very thin
1 pound firm tofu, cut into 1-inch cubes
¼-½ cup bottled fish sauce, to taste
1 pound fresh shiitake (or other, or a combination) mushrooms, stems removed and discarded and tops sliced thin
½ cup roasted peanuts
⅓ cup chopped scallions
⅓ cup chopped cilantro
1 cucumber, peeled, seeded, and cut into ½-inch dice

Roast peanuts on a baking sheet in a preheated 350°F oven for 10-15 minutes or just until golden and fragrant.

Heat the oil in a wok or heavy skillet. Add onion, garlic, ginger, and lemon grass, and sauté over medium heat until they are just browned, about 10 minutes. Stir in the tofu, fish sauce, and mushrooms, and sauté for 10 more minutes. If the mixture seems dry, add up to ½ cup water. Serve immediately, over Coconut Rice (recipe follows), sprinkled with peanuts, scallions, coriander, and cucumber.

COCONUT RICE

In Thailand this dish is made using an aromatic variety known as jasmine or "fragrant" rice, which is widely imported into the U.S. and is beginning to be grown here as well. Thai chefs use only white jasmine, but Coconut Rice is also good made with a whole grain aromatic or a long grain white rice.

2 cups jasmine rice
1 cup of coconut milk (homemade or canned, unsweetened)
3 cups water

Rinse the rice and drain it. Place a heavy pot over medium-high heat and add the well-drained rice. Toast it, stirring often at first, then constantly as it dries and begins to color, until it is fragrant and about one-third is golden brown—about 15 minutes. Pour in the coconut milk and water, stir, and bring to a boil. Immediately reduce heat to very low and cover tightly. Cook for 15-20 minutes, checking at 15, or until all liquid is absorbed. (Brown rice will take 25-30 minutes.) Fluff gently to thoroughly blend in the coconut milk, and serve.

Note: If you can't find unsweetened canned coconut milk, or would prefer to make your own, see Homemade Coconut Milk. Replace the canned coconut milk and the water here with 4 cups of homemade.

HOMEMADE COCONUT MILK

Makes 4 cups

5 cups water
5 cups dried unsweetened coconut
cheesecloth or fine mesh strainer

Boil the water and add the coconut. Let it stand for 20 minutes. Purée the coconut and its liquid 1 cup at a time in a blender at high speed for 3 minutes per batch. Pour into several layers of cheesecloth (or a thin cotton towel) resting in a strainer over a bowl. Let the coconut milk drain through the strainer. After most of the milk has drained through, gather up the cloth with the coconut in it and squeeze out the remaining milk. (If you are in a hurry, use a fine-mesh strainer—in which case the milk will be a bit pulpy.) It will keep for 4-5 days refrigerated.

THAI SHRIMP IN GREEN CURRY SAUCE OVER RICE NOODLES

Serves 4

This dish is heady with the flavors of the Far East. It goes together fast once you have made the Green Curry Sauce. We use shrimp here, but it is also good with scallops, calamari, tempeh, or tofu.

Thai noodles are made from rice flour and are very delicate. They take only seconds to cook. Three types are commonly available—*sen yai, sen lek,* and *sen mee,* or wide, medium-wide, and vermicelli, respectively. Look for rice noodles at Oriental markets and natural foods shops.

2 tablespoons sesame oil, light or dark or a combination
3 tablespoons green curry sauce (recipe follows)
1½ pounds medium shrimp, shelled and deveined
1 cup eggplant, cut into 1-inch cubes
1 sweet red pepper, cored, seeded, and sliced
½-1 teaspoon sea salt
one 8-ounce can unsweetened coconut milk (or 1 cup homemade, see
  previous recipe)
10-15 fresh basil leaves, for garnish
½ cup coarsely chopped cilantro, for garnish
1 package rice noodles

Heat oil in a wok or skillet. Add green curry sauce and stir until it bubbles. Add shrimp, eggplant, pepper, salt, and coconut milk, and stir well. Cook and stir over medium heat until the shrimp are done, about 10 minutes. To prepare rice noodles, bring 1 quart of water to a boil. Turn off the heat and add noodles. Allow to steep for 1 minute, drain quickly, and serve immediately, topped with shrimp sauce. Garnish liberally with basil and cilantro.

GREEN CURRY SAUCE

Makes ½ cup

The recipe for this spicy sauce, one of the half-dozen sauces basic to Thai cooking, comes from Thai Rama restaurant in Johnston, Rhode Island. You can use a food processor or blender to make the sauce quickly, or you can make it the traditional way with a mortar and pestle or in a suribachi (Japanese grinding bowl), which takes time, muscle power, and patience. (You may want to make a double batch and have some left over for next time. It keeps, in a covered jar in the refrigerator, for up to six months.) Try it both ways and you'll discover the difference in texture and flavor. In any event, make it well ahead of time so the flavors can blend and deepen.

*15 small green chili peppers, deseeded, deveined, and coarsely chopped
   (wear rubber gloves)*
4 stalks lemon grass, coarsely chopped (tough outer layers removed)
3 shallots, sliced thin
5 lime leaves, chopped (or grated rind of 1 lime)
1 tablespoon whole coriander seeds
1 tablespoon caraway seeds
1 tablespoon bottled fish sauce
2 tablespoons rice syrup
2 tablespoons sesame oil, light or dark or a combination

Combine all ingredients and process by hand with a mortar and pestle or in a suribachi, or in a blender or processor.

Use a dab of Green Curry Sauce anywhere you want to enliven flavor— in soups, vegetables, or grain dishes.

SHRIMP ÉTOUFFÉE

Serves 4-5

This version of a delicious Cajun dish uses shrimp instead of the usual crawfish. Serve it over fresh hot rice as a light buffet party dish.

1 pound medium shrimp
4 cups water
1 tablespoon extra virgin olive oil or light sesame oil
2 onions, sliced thin
1 cup diced green pepper
2 large ribs celery, sliced thin
½-¾ cup roux (see below)
2 teaspoons sea salt, or to taste
2-3 cloves garlic, minced
1 cup diced red bell pepper
1-2 teaspoons chopped fresh thyme, or ½-1 teaspoon dried
1 cup chopped scallions
1 cup parsley, chopped fine

ROUX

"First, make the roux...." So begin the instructions for many south Louisiana gumbos, stews, and bisques. Use it to richly thicken any savory dish.

½ cup light sesame oil or unsalted (sweet) butter
¾ cup unbleached white or whole wheat pastry flour

Heat the oil or butter in a heavy skillet until hot but not smoking. Sprinkle the flour in and stir constantly over medium heat until the roux begins to brown lightly. Keep on low-to-medium heat and stir often, until it turns the color of peanut butter. (With pastry flour the roux will be darker.) Judge by color, not time, but allow 20 minutes or so to reach the proper color. Remove from heat and let cool, continuing to stir frequently. After the roux has cooled, pour off a little of the separated oil. Leftover roux will keep indefinitely in a sealed jar in the refrigerator.

Peel and devein the shrimp, and set them aside in the refrigerator. Simmer their peelings in the water for 15 minutes. Strain, reserving this stock. Heat the oil in a heavy soup pot, and sauté the onions, green pepper, and celery for 5-8 minutes. Add the roux and salt and stir. Add the shrimp stock slowly, one cup at a time, mixing thoroughly after each addition. Add the garlic, red pepper, and thyme, and let simmer for 30-40 minutes, stirring occasionally, until thickened. Add the shrimp, scallions, and parsley, and simmer for 7-10 minutes longer, adjusting seasonings.

Chapter Five:
Salads

FRESH CORN AND RICE SALAD

Serves 5-6

Put this lovely side dish or luncheon dish together in the morning or the
night before for a slightly marinated effect.

4 cups cooked rice (any kind except sweet brown)
2 cups cooked fresh corn kernels
¼ cup extra virgin olive oil
2 tablespoons natural soy sauce
2 tablespoons brown rice vinegar
2 tablespoons mirin
1 small onion, finely grated

Combine rice and corn. Combine remaining ingredients, add to rice and
corn, and let stand at room temperature—or in the refrigerator if you'd
like it chilled—for at least 2 hours before serving. Garnish with bits of
roasted sweet red pepper (see page 50).

RICE TABOULI

Serves 4

This warm-weather grain salad is a logical variation of the familiar Middle Eastern cracked wheat salad. Have the rice—white, for best results—cooked al dente, and on the dry side.

2 cups cooked white or white aromatic rice
⅓ cup chopped scallions
2 tablespoons chopped fresh or 1 teaspoon dried mint
1 clove garlic, pressed or minced
½ cup chopped parsley
1 teaspoon chopped fresh or ½ teaspoon dried basil
1 large tomato, chopped
¼ cup fresh-squeezed lemon juice
2 tablespoons natural soy sauce
¼ cup extra virgin olive oil
whole lettuce leaves
⅓ cup halved and pitted black olives (use bulk Greek or Italian
  brine-cured rather than tinned)

Let cooked rice cool completely, then place all ingredients except lettuce leaves and olives into a bowl and toss together lightly. Chill for an hour or longer to allow flavors to blend. Wash and dry lettuce leaves, and use them to line a salad bowl. Fill with tabouli and garnish with olives.

RICE AND SHRIMP SALAD WITH
POPPY SEED DRESSING

Serves 4-6

When winter seems like it will never end, serve this lively dish to wake up hibernating taste buds.

2 cups cooked long grain brown rice
¾ cup halved string beans
1 medium carrot
6 jumbo shrimp, peeled and deveined
¼ cup sliced or chopped toasted almonds

If you make fresh rice for this, let it cool well. You can omit the shrimp and the salad will still be delicious.

Blanch the beans by boiling them for 1½ minutes, plunging them into cold water, and draining. Cut the carrot into matchsticks and blanch them, too. Cut the shrimp in half lengthwise, drop them into simmering water to cook until just tender, about 3-5 minutes, and rinse quickly with cold water. Toast almonds on a baking sheet in a preheated 350°F oven for 10-15 minutes or just until fragrant and golden.

Combine rice, beans, carrot, shrimp, and almonds, and serve on a bed of greens with Poppy Seed Dressing drizzled on.

POPPY SEED DRESSING

Makes about 1¼ cups

½ cup sunflower or olive oil
¼ cup brown rice vinegar
2 tablespoons barley malt
1 teaspoon Dijon mustard
½ teaspoon sea salt
2¼ teaspoons poppy seeds

Combine all ingredients in a jar, cover tightly, and shake well.

SUSHI SALAD

Serves 8-10

Here's a refreshing summer entrée inspired by a Japanese staple, sushi. It needs only a companionable loaf of light sourdough bread to make a meal. This recipe works better with a regular medium or long grain rice (white or brown) than with sweet brown or an aromatic rice.

1 tablespoon rice syrup
1 tablespoon toasted sesame seeds
8 cups cooked rice, cooled
3 tablespoons diced onion
4 tablespoons natural soy sauce
1 teaspoon dark sesame oil
1 teaspoon peeled and grated fresh ginger
1 teaspoon brown rice vinegar
2 cups loosely packed toasted nori, torn into bite-size bits
1 cup chopped parsley

Liquefy the rice malt syrup in a small saucepan over low heat. Toast seeds in a dry skillet or pan over medium-low heat, stirring constantly until they smell fragrant and begin to pop. Toast nori by waving the sheet over medium-low heat briefly, just until the color changes somewhat and it becomes crisp.

Combine all ingredients in a large bowl, adding nori and parsley last and reserving a handful of each for garnish.

AROMATIC RICE SALAD WITH BALSAMIC OR LEMON VINAIGRETTE

Serves 4

The rich flavor and smell of aromatic rice makes this salad memorable. On a sweltering summer day it's light and refreshing, yet substantial enough for a dinner entrée. For an interesting variation, use fennel bulb instead of celery. (For the best flavor, choose the flatter-shaped bulbs.)

2 cups cooked aromatic rice
½ cup minced red onion
½ cup diced yellow banana pepper (or other sweet pepper)
½ cup coarsely chopped unsalted pistachio nuts or unsalted toasted cashews
½ cup chopped fennel or celery

BALSAMIC OR LEMON VINAIGRETTE

½ cup balsamic vinegar or lemon juice
⅛ teaspoon umeboshi vinegar
½ cup extra virgin olive oil
1 tablespoon natural soy sauce
½ teaspoon sea salt
1 tablespoon fresh oregano leaves or 1 teaspoon dried

Combine rice, onion, pepper, nuts, and fennel in a large bowl. In a small bowl combine the dressing ingredients and mix. Toss salad with the dressing and chill for an hour. To serve, make a bed of a dozen washed red lettuce leaves and top with the salad.

WARM WILD RICE SALAD WITH
HERB VINAIGRETTE

Serves 8-9

Lightly dressed, this tweedy-looking salad can serve as a grain-and-vegetable main dish.

HERB VINAIGRETTE

¼ cup light nut or seed oil, such as sesame or walnut
3 tablespoons brown rice vinegar
1 clove garlic, minced
¾ teaspoon sea salt
pinch black pepper
½ teaspoon dried marjoram
¼ teaspoon dried thyme
pinch dried rosemary

Combine dressing ingredients and shake well in a jar or process in a blender. Allow to stand so that flavors can blend while the rice cooks.

WARM WILD RICE SALAD

2 cups water
1 cup broccoli, top cut into small florets, stem thinly sliced, tough
  bottom discarded
½ cup thinly sliced carrot rounds
4 dried shiitake mushrooms
1 leek, white part only, sliced into thin rounds
¼ cup minced parsley
¼ cup thinly sliced scallions
½ cup toasted and coarsely chopped pecans or walnuts

1 cup wild rice
1 cup long grain or aromatic rice
3 cups vegetable stock or water
1 tablespoon natural soy sauce

Bring the water to a boil in a two-quart pot, drop in the broccoli, carrot, mushrooms, and leek, and cook until just tender, about 3-5 minutes. Drain, reserving the broth, and set the vegetables aside. Cut off the mushroom stems and discard, and slice the caps thinly.

Rinse the rices and drain. Place the vegetable broth in a pot with enough water to measure 3 cups. Add the soy sauce and bring to a boil. Add rices and mushrooms and smooth the surface with a wooden spoon. When boiling resumes, turn heat to low and cook, covered, for 1 hour, placing a flame tamer under the pot halfway through.

To serve, fluff the rice into a serving bowl, alternating with layers of cooked and raw vegetables and the nuts. Drizzle with dressing. For variety, add celery, or, during the summer, fresh corn, peas, and yellow and green summer squash. Use pine nuts, almonds, or pumpkin seeds.

THAI CALAMARI SALAD WITH FRESH PEAS

Serves 4-6

You can find calamari—squid—already cleaned and sliced at fish markets or in the frozen food department of many supermarkets.

1 pound calamari rings, thawed
2 cups fresh peas, shelled (or use frozen peas)
1 large onion, quartered and sliced thin
4 cloves garlic, minced
1 cup sliced water chestnuts
2 tomatoes, cut into l-inch dice
½ cup dark sesame oil
½ cup brown rice vinegar
1 teaspoon umeboshi vinegar
½-1 teaspoon sea salt
1 teaspoon curry powder
1 teaspoon cumin seeds
pinch cayenne powder, or to taste

Bring 1 quart of water to a boil. Add calamari and cook for 2 minutes; add peas and cook for 3 minutes more. (If you are using frozen peas, cook according to package direction. Prepare the calamari separately, cooking it for 5 minutes.) Drain and rinse in cold water. Place in a bowl and add the remaining ingredients. Mix well, and serve chilled or at room temperature.

SZECHUAN SALAD WITH HOT PEPPER SAUCE DRESSING

Serves 4

A refreshing, intensely flavored salad reminiscent of fiery Chinese Szechuan-style cooking—a good side dish with fish.

Rice vermicelli is also called "cellophane noodles," because that's exactly what it looks like. Usually made from white rice, it has a surprising texture, and though by itself it is short on flavor, in a zesty salad or soup it makes for an unusual dish.

5 ounces rice vermicelli
2 cups snow peas, stem ends and veins removed
½ cup carrot, cut into thin rounds
1 bunch watercress, roughly chopped into 1-inch pieces
2 cups mung bean sprouts
½ cup hot pepper sauce dressing (see below)

Bring 6 cups of water to a boil, add vermicelli, and remove from heat. Let stand briefly, just until tender. Drain, rinse under cold water, and set aside. Bring to a boil 4 cups water, add a pinch of sea salt, and individually parboil the snow peas, carrot, watercress, and finally the bean sprouts: drop vegetables into boiling water and cook just until colors brighten (for bean sprouts, just until translucent), 1-2 minutes. Drain, and toss gently with the noodles.

HOT PEPPER SAUCE DRESSING

Makes ½ cup

2 tablespoons lemon juice
2 tablespoons umeboshi vinegar
1 teaspoon bottled hot pepper sauce
¼ cup dark sesame oil

Combine first three ingredients, then whisk in the oil. Pour over salad and toss gently.

AMAZAKE SALAD DRESSING

Makes 1-1½ cups

The sweetest of all rices is the plump-grained glutinous variety, "sweet rice." The Japanese know how to make it even sweeter, by combining it with a grain or bean that has been inoculated with spores of a strain of *Aspergillus* mold and then letting it ferment lightly. The result is amazake, whose delicate sweetness derives only from grain and natural fermentation—which carries with it the added benefit of being good for us.

Similar to a creamy Italian, this slightly sweet yet tart dressing makes a tossed salad sing. The use of two oils is for no other reason than that it works.

> ½ cup amazake (see page 92)
> 2 tablespoons light sesame oil
> 2 tablespoons extra virgin olive oil
> ¼ cup brown rice vinegar or white wine vinegar
> 1 tablespoon red miso
> 1 clove garlic, sliced

Combine all ingredients in a blender and process until smooth. Serve on tossed green salads or pasta salads. Garnish salad with croutons or toasted seeds or chopped nuts.

AMAZAKE SUMMER PICKLES

Naturally fermented, pickles aid digestion and provide important nutrients. They are also delicious, and go with just about everything except dessert. In winter, salty "long-time" pickles are in order, but summer calls for a refreshing, light, quick pickle.

This simple amazake one works on all counts. Once you have made the pickling mix, store it in the refrigerator. Two or three hours before a meal, choose complementary pickle vegetables. Clean them, slice them, and coat them with pickling mix. Set them aside at room temperature, and you will have healthful, tasty pickles in time for dinner and custom-made for it. Also try these in sandwiches and salads.

1 cup amazake (see page 92)
1 tablespoon sea salt
vegetables of choice

Place amazake in a saucepan and bring it slowly to a simmer, stirring frequently to prevent scorching. Remove from heat and allow to cool to room temperature. Mix in the salt. Store in a covered jar in the refrigerator.

Some favorite vegetables for this pickle are carrots, cucumber, daikon, red radish, and turnip, but many others work well. Experiment, and find your own favorites, but make several different-colored ones at once in separate bowls. Slice each vegetable thinly and toss it well with enough pickling mix to thoroughly coat each slice. Set aside until mealtime (dense-textured vegetables, such as carrots, daikon, and turnips, may take longer, unless sliced very thinly).

To serve, shake off excess pickling mix and arrange the pickles attractively in a pickle dish or on a small plate. Refrigerate leftover pickles, and munch them later for a cooling tidbit.

Much of the salt will have been drawn from used pickling mix, and it will be diluted by water from the vegetables. You can combine this with an equal amount of fresh mixture and use it for pickling again, or add it to bread and muffin recipes.

GINGER PICKLES

Makes 2 cups

The sushi you order at a Japanese restaurant comes with a little pile of thinly sliced pickled ginger. The sweet-tangy taste and delicate crispness are perfect with rice and fish. Make it yourself, without the artificial coloring and white sugar, and serve it as a delicious and unusual condiment with grain dishes and fish.

1½ cups ginger, sliced as thinly as possible (if it is fresh and firm, with a
*   shiny light-brown skin, you need not peel it)*
½ cup brown rice vinegar
½ cup natural soy sauce
½ cup mirin or dry cooking sherry
½ cup rice syrup
½ cup water

Bring vinegar, tamari, mirin, syrup, and water to a boil in a heavy non-aluminum saucepan. Add ginger, reduce heat, and simmer for 5 minutes. Remove from heat and let cool before storing in a covered jar in the refrigerator. It will keep for up to four months.

Note: The best ginger for pickles is the fresh young ginger available in the spring. It should be firm and juicy, with a taut, unwrinkled skin.

Chapter Six:
Desserts and Beverages

SWEDISH ALMOND RICE PUDDING

Serves 6-8

This rice pudding—here made creamy with tofu—is a Christmas tradition in Scandinavia. One almond is hidden in the dish, and the lucky one who finds it gets the "almond present," usually a little marzipan figure.

1 cup whole almonds
1½ cups water
pinch sea salt
2 teaspoons agar flakes
4 tablespoons rice syrup
1 cup crumbled soft-style tofu
½ cup almond butter
vanilla extract
3 cups cooked brown or white rice

Blanch the almonds by dropping them into boiling water to cover and cooking for 1 minute. Drain, rinse with cool water, and slip off skins. Set aside 10 whole almonds. Chop the rest, and spread them on a baking sheet. Toast in a preheated 350°F oven for 5-10 minutes or just until golden and fragrant.

Place the 1½ cups water into a pot, add salt and rice malt, and sprinkle the agar flakes over. Bring to a simmer, stirring constantly, and cook for 10 minutes. Stir in the tofu and almond butter and cook for 3 minutes more. Purée the mixture in a blender, add a dash of vanilla, and combine with the rice and chopped almonds. Hide 1 whole almond in the pudding as you turn it out into an attractive casserole. Let cool, and decorate with the remaining almonds.

KHEER
(Indian Rice Pudding)

Serves 8-10

Exotic and ambrosial, this lovely dessert is said to have been the Buddha's first food after his epic fasting meditation.

1 cup aromatic rice
2 cups water
pinch sea salt
2 cups almonds, blanched (see previous recipe)
1 cup water
3-4 cups plain soymilk
¼ cup maple syrup
½ teaspoon each cinnamon, cardamom, and clove powder; or 2
* cinnamon sticks, 6 green whole cardamom pods, and 10 whole cloves*
* with round tops removed*
a few strands of saffron (optional)
½ cup seedless raisins
½ cup cashews

Wash rice and drain. Combine with water and salt and bring to a boil. Lower flame, cover, and simmer until the rice is soft and the water has been absorbed.

Place the blanched almonds in a blender with the cup of water and process to a smooth, thick liquid. (You may need to process in batches, using a little more water as necessary.) Add the almond mash to the rice in a pot with the soymilk and place over medium-low heat. Cook for 10-15 minutes, stirring out any lumps and adding more soymilk or water if necessary to prevent scorching. Reduce heat to low, add the remaining ingredients, and cook, stirring often, for 20-30 minutes more. Taste for sweetness and add more maple syrup if you like. Serve warm or cool.

AMAZAKE CUSTARD

Serves 4

2 cups mocha or strawberry amazake shake (see page 95 or 96)
2-3 tablespoons rice syrup or maple syrup, to taste
1½ tablespoons agar flakes
2 tablespoons kuzu (crush chunks before measuring)
1 teaspoon vanilla extract

In a medium saucepan combine the amazake beverage and syrup. Sprinkle the agar flakes on, and bring to a simmer over medium heat, stirring gently until agar is dissolved. Thoroughly dissolve the kuzu in 2 tablespoons cold water and add it to the pan while stirring briskly. Simmer for 2 minutes, stirring constantly while the mixture thickens. Remove from heat and stir in the vanilla. Pour into custard cups or small bowls and chill until firm before serving, about 2 hours. Garnish with fresh berries, toasted coconut, or slivered toasted almonds.

AMAZAKE

(Sweet Rice Pudding, Beverage, or Sweetener)

Makes 8-10 cups

In Japan amazake has been served for centuries as a warming winter toddy, spiked with ginger. Western cooks who have discovered it consider it one of Japan's living national treasures, and use it in a variety of dishes where a simple delicate sweetness is wanted—from desserts to pickles. The recipes in this book demonstrate the scope of amazake's versatility and serve as an inspiration for you to invent your own.

It is easy to find packaged commercial amazake in natural foods shops, but if you have the time, consider learning the simple art of making your own. Amazake keeps well in the refrigerator, so you can make a batch every couple of weeks or so to have on hand when the muses inspire you.

Ask for koji (the "starter"—a grain, usually white rice, inoculated with the *Aspergillus* mold) at natural foods shops, and store it tightly covered in the refrigerator. In the freezer it will keep indefinitely.

The recipe calls for sweet rice, but you can use half sweet rice and half any of the brown or white rices, or even another grain—once you have the technique, experiment!

3 cups sweet rice
7 cups water
1 cup koji rice

Wash sweet rice and place in a pressure cooker with the water. Bring up to pressure and cook for 60 minutes. (If pot-boiling, use 8-9 cups of water and cover tightly. Cooking time might be a little longer for the grains to become completely broken and tender.) Remove from heat, let pressure come down, and turn out into a glass or ceramic bowl. Let cool to approximately 100°F (when steam no longer rises from the rice and you can leave your inserted finger in and it feels hot but not unbearable). Add koji and mix thoroughly. Cover the bowl with a bamboo sushi mat or other porous cover and let it sit at room temperature for 8-10 hours, stirring occasionally.

The longer you let the amazake ferment, the sweeter it will be. Be careful not to let it sour, though. When it is "done," transfer it back to the cooking pot, bring it slowly to a simmer, and add a pinch of salt to stop the fermenting action. Simmer for a few minutes, stirring frequently, then remove from heat.

Eat amazake as a pudding, fresh, hot, and plain; eat it for breakfast, with a sprinkling of granola or nuts; use it as the sweetener-liquid in baked goods, pancakes, and waffles; or use it in any of the following ways.

AMAZAKE TODDY

For a hot, creamy cup of comfort on a chilly day, combine one part amazake with 1-1½ parts water. If you prefer a smooth consistency, purée it in a blender. Transfer to a saucepan and bring just to a simmer, stirring occasionally. Enhance amazake's ambrosial flavor by adding a pinch of finely grated fresh ginger just before serving, or try it with a small pinch of nutmeg and a few drops of vanilla extract. Cooled to room temperature, or slightly chilled, it makes a delicious summer drink.

ALMOND AMAZAKE SHAKE

Makes 1 pint

The key to the richness of this delicious drink is the almond butter. Ground toasted almonds just don't do the trick. Although it is a little less convenient than the soymilk option, almond milk is best here.

1 cup amazake
1½ cups almond milk (recipe follows) or ½ to ¾ cup each plain
  soymilk and water
2-3 tablespoons almond butter
2 tablespoons rice syrup
small pinch sea salt
½ teaspoon vanilla extract
⅛ teaspoon almond extract

Combine all ingredients in a blender and purée thoroughly. Serve the shake well chilled.

ALMOND MILK

Makes 1 quart

1 cup raw almonds
4 cups cold water
⅛ teaspoon sea salt
1 tablespoon light sesame or corn oil (optional)
2 tablespoons rice syrup (optional)

Drop almonds into boiling water to cover and cook for 1 minute. Drain, let cool somewhat, and slip off skins.

Combine blanched almonds with the measured water and remaining ingredients in a blender and process for 1-2 minutes. Strain through a double layer of cheesecloth, and squeeze out all liquid.

Almond milk will keep for about six days if stored in a covered container in the refrigerator. You can use it much as you would cow's milk. Save the almond meal in a covered container in the refrigerator, and use it when you make cookies, pie crusts, or bread.

STRAWBERRY AMAZAKE SHAKE

Makes about 3 cups

1 cup amazake
2 cups fresh or frozen strawberries (thawed)
1 cup soymilk or almond milk (see previous recipe)
¼ teaspoon vanilla extract
2 tablespoons rice syrup or maple syrup, to taste

Purée all ingredients thoroughly in a blender. If you want a creamy texture, pour through a fine-mesh strainer to remove rice hulls and strawberry seeds. Serve well chilled, garnished with a sprig of mint.

MOCHA AMAZAKE SHAKE

Makes 1 pint

1 cup amazake
1-1½ cups almond milk (see page 94) or ½ to ¾ cup each soymilk and
  water
2 tablespoons instant grain coffee powder
2 tablespoons cocoa powder
2 tablespoons rice syrup or maple syrup or half and half
pinch sea salt
½ teaspoon vanilla extract

Proceed as for Almond Amazake Shake (see page 94). Serve hot or cold, with a sprinkling of freshly grated nutmeg.

Note: It's easy and fun to make amazake Popsicles by blending a little extra sweetener into this or any of the preceding amazake shakes. Pour into Popsicle molds or small paper cups and let freeze until solid, putting sticks in when the mixture is half frozen.

AMAZAKE PECAN PIE

Makes one 9- or 10-inch pie

CRUST

¾ cup whole wheat pastry flour
¾ cup unbleached white flour
pinch sea salt
pinch cinnamon
¼ cup corn oil, chilled
½-¾ cup water, very cold

Chill oil and water in separate containers in the freezer for 30-45 minutes.

Preheat oven to 375°F. Combine flours, salt, and cinnamon, then cut oil in with a fork to a pebbly consistency. Quickly mix the water in, gather dough into a ball, and roll out on a lightly floured surface. Fit dough into a lightly greased pie plate, flute edges, prick bottom with a fork, and bake for 15-20 minutes or until golden brown and done.

FILLING

3 cups amazake
½ teaspoon sea salt
1½ tablespoons agar flakes
2 tablespoons kuzu (crush before measuring), dissolved in ¼ cup water
2 cups shelled pecan halves
½ cup barley malt syrup
½ cup maple syrup

In a two-quart saucepan combine amazake, salt, and agar flakes. Bring slowly to a boil, stirring constantly, then reduce heat to simmer. Cook for 5 minutes, stirring often, until the agar dissolves. Add the kuzu and cook, stirring constantly, until the mixture thickens. Remove from heat and allow to cool somewhat before pouring into prebaked shell. Refrigerate for 30 minutes.

Arrange pecans on top of the pie. Combine syrups and pour over the pie. Refrigerate for 30 more minutes, or until completely set.

RICE AND FALL FRUIT PIE

Serve this unusual hearty pie as an accompaniment to a light meal, or as a special snack.

½ cup toasted, chopped almonds
3 apples
2 ripe peaches or pears
2 teaspoons lemon juice
1 teaspoon vanilla extract
pinch sea salt
pinch cinnamon
¼ cup apple juice
¼ cup light soymilk
½ cup maple syrup
1 tablespoon red wine
1 tablespoon almond butter (or another nut or seed butter)
2 cups cooked brown rice
1 tablespoon arrowroot, dissolved in 2 tablespoons water
1 prebaked 10-inch pie shell (or see previous recipe)
10 dried apricots, almond slivers, and mint leaves for garnish

Toast almonds on a baking sheet in a preheated 350°F oven until just golden and fragrant, about 10-15 minutes. Peel, core, and slice the apples. Pit and slice the peaches (or core and slice the pears). Toss fruit with lemon juice, vanilla, salt, and cinnamon. Place the fruit, apple juice, soymilk, maple syrup, and red wine in a pot and cook for about 5 minutes, until the apples are soft. Mix in the nut or seed butter, rice, and arrowroot mixture. Stir constantly for 2 minutes or until the mixture thickens. Remove from heat, chop and add the toasted almonds, and fill the prebaked pie shell. Let the pie cool completely before slicing. Slice the dried apricots and use as garnish along with almond slivers and mint leaves.

RICE AND OAT CARROT MUFFINS

Makes 12

1 cup soymilk
¼ teaspoon cider vinegar or brown rice vinegar
1 cup rice flour
1 cup oat flour (process oatmeal in a blender or coffee mill, then measure)
1 teaspoon baking soda
1 teaspoon baking powder
½ teaspoon sea salt
1 teaspoon cinnamon
½ cup maple syrup
1½ teaspoons vanilla extract
⅓ cup light oil
2 cups grated carrot
½ cup chopped walnuts
½ cup raisins

Combine soymilk and vinegar and set aside. Preheat oven to 350°F Lightly grease muffin tins.

Mix the dry ingredients together. In a separate bowl combine syrup and vanilla, add soymilk-vinegar, and mix. Gradually whisk in the oil. Add the wet mixture to the dry, lightly stir in carrots, walnuts, and raisins, and spoon immediately into muffin tins and place in the oven. Bake for 30 minutes or until an inserted toothpick comes out clean.

AMAZAKE SCONES

Makes about 18 three-inch pastries

The British invented scones to eat with their afternoon tea. They know that for best results you should handle the dough as little as possible. It's also crucial to get the scones into the oven quickly once the leavening agents are mixed with the liquid ingredients. Serve scones still warm and with butter and jam. It is nearly impossible to find a scone before three in the afternoon in the British Isles, but at home we can make and eat them whenever we like.

If your scones turn out flat at first, they will still be delicious. Keep trying, and you'll develop the right touch.

¼ cup plain soymilk
¼ teaspoon cider vinegar or brown rice vinegar
½ cup amazake (see page 92)
⅓ cup currants or finely chopped raisins
2 teaspoons finely grated lemon zest (optional)
1½ cups whole wheat pastry flour
½ cup unbleached white flour
½ teaspoon sea salt
2 teaspoons baking powder
½ teaspoon baking soda
1½ teaspoons cinnamon
¼ cup melted butter

Combine soymilk and vinegar and let sit for 5 minutes. Preheat the oven to 400°F, and butter two baking sheets.

Combine soymilk-vinegar with amazake in a blender and process until fairly smooth. Pour into a small bowl and add the dried fruit and lemon zest. Sift the dry ingredients into a bowl and mix well. Add the melted butter and cut it in quickly with a fork until the mixture is pebbly.

Make a well in the center of the flour mixture. Add liquid ingredients, and mix lightly with your fork just until the flour is moist. Knead the dough quickly and gently a couple of times to form a ball. The dough should be soft and slightly sticky. If it seems too sticky you can mix in a little more flour, if too dry, a bit more water. (When you make them again, try to get the proportions just right so you can omit this rescuing step—any extra working of the dough lessens chances for a tender scone.)

On a floured board, quickly press or roll the dough out to ½-inch thickness. Cut rounds with a biscuit cutter or a glass and place them on the baking sheets. Bake for 10-15 minutes. Scones should be golden when done, and still soft.

RICE AND WALNUT FRUIT PANCAKES

Makes ten 3½-inch pancakes

1¾ cups light soymilk (a brand made without oil)
1¾ teaspoons cider vinegar
2 cups rice flour
1 cup whole wheat flour
¼ teaspoon sea salt
1 tablespoon baking soda
2 eggs
¾ cup water
¼ cup maple syrup
1 teaspoon vanilla extract
2 tablespoons canola oil
⅓ cup chopped walnuts
1 cup chopped fresh fruit (strawberries, bananas, and peaches are delicious)
oil or butter for cooking

Combine soymilk and vinegar and set aside for 5 minutes. Combine the dry ingredients. In a separate bowl combine the wet, including soymilk-vinegar. Lightly stir in the walnuts and fruit.

Place a skillet over medium heat and add enough oil or butter to liberally coat. When a drop of batter sizzles on the pan, pour on the batter, ¼ cup for each pancake. Cook until golden on each side. Add more oil or butter to the pan as needed.

Serve pancakes piping hot, with maple syrup or yogurt.

CHOCOLATE-CHOCOLATE CHIP CAKE
WITH MOCHA CUSTARD FILLING

Serves 16-24

This cake would stimulate any chocolate lover's taste buds. Since it calls for rice flour and oat flour, it can be enjoyed by people who are wheat-sensitive. If you can't find oat flour, process oatmeal in a blender or coffee mill before measuring. A coffee flavored liqueur such as Kahlua is optional but does add a wonderful flavor.

MOCHA CUSTARD FILLING

2¼ cups light vanilla flavored soymilk
6 tablespoons maple syrup
2 tablespoons coffee flavored liqueur (optional)
pinch sea salt
1½ tablespoons agar flakes
2 tablespoons grain beverage
1 tablespoon unsweetened cocoa powder
1 teaspoon vanilla extract
2 tablespoons kuzu, dissolved in 2 tablespoons cool water

Combine soymilk, maple syrup, liqueur, and salt in a small saucepan. Sprinkle the agar flakes over the mixture. Without stirring, bring to a simmer over medium heat. Simmer 2-5 minutes, until the flakes have dissolved, stirring occasionally. Add the grain beverage, cocoa, and vanilla, and mix well until all of the ingredients are combined. Add the kuzu-water mixture and stir continuously until the mixture thickens, 2-5 minutes. Remove from heat and pour into a bowl. Chill custard thoroughly. The quickest method is to put it in the freezer, uncovered, until it is firm, about 45 minutes.

CHOCOLATE-CHOCOLATE CHIP CAKE

½ cup toasted, chopped walnuts
butter for cake pans
⅓ cup unflavored soymilk
1 cup rice flour
½ cup oat flour
½ teaspoon sea salt
1 teaspoon baking powder
1 tablespoon arrowroot powder
2 cups malt-sweetened chocolate chips
⅓ cup unsalted butter or ⅓ cup canola oil
⅓ cup maple syrup
1 teaspoon vanilla extract
2 eggs

Before chopping them, toast the walnuts on a baking sheet in a preheated 350°F oven until just golden and fragrant, about 10-15 minutes.

Keeping the oven at 350°F, generously butter two 9-inch round cake pans.

Mix together the walnuts, flours, salt, baking powder, arrowroot, and 1 cup of the chocolate chips in a bowl. Melt the second cup of chocolate chips with the ⅓ cup butter in a double boiler. (If you're not using the butter, melt the chocolate chips in the double-boiler and add the oil to the wet ingredients.) In a separate bowl whisk together the maple syrup, eggs, soymilk, and vanilla. Add the melted chocolate mixture, whisking to combine thoroughly. Add the wet mixture to the dry, stirring until thoroughly blended. Pour into the pan, and bake for 25-30 minutes, just until an inserted toothpick comes out clean. Let cool for 20 minutes on a rack before removing from the pan. The rice flour makes the cake quite delicate, so it needs to be handled with care. Cool it almost to room temperature before turning it out of the pan.

CHOCOLATE ICING

4 ounces unsweetened baking chocolate
2 tablespoons unsalted butter
½ cup light vanilla soymilk
pinch sea salt
¾ cup maple syrup
1 tablespoon plus 1 teaspoon kuzu, dissolved in 2 tablespoons cool
  water
1 teaspoon vanilla extract
1 tablespoon coffee flavored liqueur (optional)
strawberry slivers to garnish

Melt chocolate and butter in one-quart saucepan over very low heat. Remove from heat and add the soymilk, salt, and maple syrup. Return to medium heat and add kuzu-water mixture. Stir continuously until the mixture thickens. Remove from heat, add coffee liqueur and vanilla, and mix well. Allow mixture to cool to lukewarm before icing the cake.

To assemble cake, place one layer of the cake on a flat surface and spread with a ½ -inch layer of the chilled Mocha Custard. Leave about a ¼ -inch margin around the edge of the cake. Carefully place second layer of cake on top of first. Cover the entire cake with chocolate icing. If there is leftover custard, fill a decorating bag and decorate the cake with it, or garnish with strawberry slivers.

SWEET RICE AND NUT BALLS

Makes 18-20

Add these delicately sweet treats to a winter holiday platter.

1½ cups sweet rice
2 cups water
pinch sea salt
2½ cups coarsely chopped roasted walnuts
¼ cup raisins
¼ teaspoon cinnamon

Wash rice and drain. Place in pressure cooker with water and salt, bring up to pressure, and cook for 45 minutes. Remove from heat and let pressure drop completely. Open cooker, stir rice, and let cool for about 10 minutes. Note: To pot-boil, use 2½ cups of water and cook for 60 minutes or until rice is tender and glutinous. Pressure-cooking works best here, though, since you want the rice to be sticky.

Before chopping them, toast the walnuts on a baking sheet in a preheated 350°F oven until just golden and fragrant, about 10-15 minutes. Mix the raisins and cinnamon into half of the rice and grind the mixture in a grinder or mix well with a wooden spoon. Combine remaining rice with the ground mixture and mix well. Moisten your hands with water, form the mixture into bite-size balls, and roll each in the chopped nuts.

ALMOND RICE CRISPIES

Makes 9-12 bars

These make a sweet lunch box or after-school treat.

¾ cup chopped toasted almonds
¾ cup rice syrup
1 teaspoon vanilla extract
2 cups brown rice crispies
2 tablespoons tahini or sesame butter

Toast almonds on a baking sheet in a preheated 350°F oven until just golden and fragrant, about 10-15 minutes. Grind to a meal in a food processor or blender. In a small saucepan heat the rice syrup to a simmer. Combine syrup, almonds, and vanilla in a bowl and mix well. Add rice crispies and tahini or sesame butter and mix well. Press the mixture into a lightly oiled or buttered 6½ -inch cake pan and let set or refrigerate for a few hours before cutting.

STRAWBERRY OR RASPBERRY SORBET

Makes about 1½ pints (3 cups)

A sorbet is a refreshing frozen fruit dessert with a smooth texture. A little wine makes it creamy.

16 ounces fresh or frozen unsweetened strawberries or raspberries, juice
*   included*
⅓ cup water
2 level teaspoons agar flakes
⅔-1 cup rice syrup (use larger measurement with very tart frozen
*   raspberries)*
2-3 tablespoons blush wine such as White Zinfandel
1 teaspoon lemon juice

Purée the berries (thaw first, if frozen) in a blender or food processor. Press through a fine mesh strainer to remove seeds.

Sprinkle the agar flakes over the water in a small pan, and slowly bring to a simmer over low heat. Simmer gently for 3 minutes, stirring occasionally. Remove from heat, and stir in the rice syrup, wine, and lemon juice. Combine syrup mixture and berry purée, and pour into a baking pan, casserole, or undivided ice cube tray. Cover with foil or plastic wrap and freeze until solid.

When it is frozen, scrape the mixture with a fork until it resembles finely crushed ice. Working quickly, spoon half the mixture into a chilled food processor bowl or blender, and process briefly, just until light and smooth but not thawed. Process the other half. Serve immediately, or, for a firmer texture, place the blended sorbet in a container, cover, and refreeze for 1-3 hours (if allowed to freeze longer it will become too hard).

Note: You can also process the sorbet in an ice cream maker.

Glossary

Look for these and any other unfamiliar products at well-stocked natural foods shops and Oriental markets. Many supermarkets now carry ethnic, gourmet, and natural foods.

ADUKI BEANS—small red Japanese beans

AGAR FLAKES—gelatin derived from a sea vegetable, also known as kanten

AMAZAKE—a sweet, thick nonalcoholic fermented rice drink from Japan

ARBORIO—a medium grain rice popular in Italy

AROMATIC RICE—any of a variety of brown or white rices with a fragrant, nutty aroma, such as basmati, Wehani, and Texmati; also known as scented rice

ARROWROOT POWDER—a vegetable starch thickener

BARLEY MALT—a sweet, thick, dark brown syrup made from sprouted barley

BASMATI—a light, flavorful aromatic rice, native to India and Pakistan

BONITO FLAKES—shaved dried fish

BROWN RICE—rice with the tough outer husk removed but otherwise the whole grain left; also known as whole rice; may be gold, cream-colored, or red in addition to brown

BROWN RICE VINEGAR—a full-bodied yet mild seasoning, not as sharp as other vinegars

BURDOCK—an earthy flavored edible root cultivated primarily in Japan

CHINESE 5-SPICE—a packaged Chinese "curry powder," a combination of peppers and spices

DAIKON—a large Japanese icicle-type radish

DARK SESAME OIL—a strong-tasting oil made from sesame seeds that were roasted before being pressed; also known as "roasted" or "toasted" sesame oil

FISH SAUCE—a strongly flavored Oriental condiment, usually made with water, anchovy extract, and salt

GHEE—clarified butter, from India

HERBAMARE—a packaged seasoning made from sea salt, kelp, and herbs

HOT PEPPER OIL—bottled roasted (dark) sesame oil flavored with red chili pepper

JASMINE—a long grain aromatic rice variety from Thailand

KOMBU—an edible sea vegetable, also known as kelp

KUZU—a vegetable starch used as a thickener

LONG GRAIN RICE—a mostly tropical variety, it cooks up drier and fluffier than shorter grains; a good choice when each grain should be distinguishable in a dish, such as a salad or pilaf

MIRIN—Japanese sweet cooking wine

MISO—a Japanese fermented soy, grain, and salt product, made in varieties ranging from light and mild to dark and very salty

MOCHI—sticky, sweet brown rice that's been soaked, steamed, and pounded into a block; a traditional Japanese product

NATURAL SOY SAUCE—traditional soy sauce, a soybean and salt product made without artificial ingredients; can be either shoyu (contains wheat) or tamari (made without wheat)

NORI—an edible sea vegetable

PADDY RICE—rice in its raw state, with the inedible husk still on it; also known as rough rice

PARBOILED RICE—rice that has been soaked, steamed, and dried to drive the water-soluble nutrients of the bran into the endosperm where they are preserved during milling; also known as "converted" or "precooked" rice

PESTO—a fresh herb, garlic, olive oil, lemon juice, and nut or seed mixture used as a condiment and sauce

PILAF—a grain dish in which the grain is first heated in a pan, dry or with oil, and then combined with liquid and cooked

QUINOA—(pronounced keen-wa) a hearty, nutritious grain grown by the Incas and "rediscovered" by North Americans within the past ten years

RICE SYRUP—a thick, sweet syrup made from whole grain rice and used as a sweetener; also known as rice malt

SEA SALT—unrefined salt still with its trace minerals

SEITAN—the gluten of wheat that has been separated from the bran and starch and then cooked and richly flavored in a broth of ginger, soy sauce, and kombu sea vegetable; also known as wheat meat

S H I I T A K E —Japanese forest mushrooms, available dry or fresh

S H O Y U —a natural soy sauce, made from soybeans, wheat, and salt

S O Y M I L K —processed soy beverage, available in a variety of flavors and thicknesses

S U R I B A C H I —Japanese textured grinding bowl with wooden pestle

T A B O U L I —a Middle Eastern salad made with bulgur and usually tomatoes, onion, mint, olive oil, and lemon juice

T A H I N I —finely ground sesame seed paste, from the Middle East

T A M A R I —a natural soy sauce, made from soybeans and salt, without wheat

T E M P E H —a fermented split soybean product from Indonesia

T O F U —soybean curd, popular throughout the Orient

U M E B O S H I   P A S T E —mashed salt-pickled Japanese plums

U M E B O S H I   V I N E G A R —the liquid from salt-pickled Japanese plums

W H I T E   R I C E —rice that's been milled and polished to remove all the bran layers and the germ

W H O L E   R I C E —(see brown rice)

W I L D   R I C E —not actually a rice but the seed of an aquatic grass

Resources

MAIL-ORDER SOURCES

Various types of rice and a wide variety of other natural foods can be obtained through the mail from the following companies. Many retail natural foods stores will also make mail-order sales. Contact stores or the following companies for catalogs or further information.

Diamond K Enterprises
R.R. 1, Box 30
St. Charles, MN 55972
(507) 932-4308

Garden Spot Distributors
438 White Oak Rd.
New Holland, PA 17557
(800) 829-5100

Goldmine Natural Food Company
1947 30th St.
San Diego, CA 92102
(800) 475-3663

Green Earth Natural Foods
2545 Prairie St.
Evanston, IL 60201
(800) 322-3662

Jaffe Bros.
P.O. Box 636
Valley Center, CA 92082
(619) 749-1133

Lundberg Family Farms
P.O. Box 369
Richvale, CA 95974
(916) 882-4551

Minnesota Hand Harvested Wild Rice Association
Box 1903
Bemidji, MN 56601
(218) 246-8843

Mountain Ark Trading Co.
120 South East Ave.
Fayetteville, AR 72701
(800) 643-8909

Texmati Rice
P.O. Box 1305
Alvin, TX 77512
(800) 232-7423

Timber Crest Farms
4791 Dry Creek
Healdsburg, CA 95448
(707) 433-8251

Walnut Acres
Walnut Acres Rd.
Penns Creek, PA 17862
(800) 433-3998

BOOKS

The Rice Diet Report by Judy Moscovitz, Avon Books, 1987, 210 pages, paperback, $4.50.

Rice by Bonnie Tandy Leblang and Joanne Lamb Hayes, Harmony Books, 1991, 134 pages, hardcover, $11.00.

Shopper's Guide to Natural Foods from the Editors of East West/Natural Health, Avery Publishing Group, 1987, 204 pages, paperback, $12.95.

About the Author

Natural Health is a pioneering bimonthly magazine whose readers now number in excess of 450,000. Formerly titled *East West: The Journal of Natural Health and Living,* the magazine celebrated its twentieth anniversary in 1991 and has gained a national reputation for its coverage of issues relating to whole foods and alternative health. It was recently listed as one of only three "most-asked-for-magazines" in the health and nutrition category by *The New York Public Library Desk Reference.* In 1989 it won an Alternative Press Award for Service Journalism, and was a finalist in 1990 for Best Publication Over 50,000 and Feature Writing awards, and in 1991 for Service Journalism. The editors of *Natural Health* have authored a number of popular natural foods cookbooks and the definitive *Shopper's Guide to Natural Foods.* The magazine is produced in Brookline, Massachusetts, by a staff of twenty.

THE NATURAL HEALTH BOOKSHELF

Shop from home for the best guides to natural foods, holistic health, and whole foods cooking.

Order now toll-free: (800) 876-1001 Mon-Fri 9am-5pm EST. Visa and MasterCard accepted. Or order directly by mailing check or money order to Natural Health Books, P.O. Box 1200, 17 Station St., Brookline Village, MA 02147. Include $3.00 postage and handling for first book and $0.50 for each additional book.

Seven Steps to Better Vision: Easy, Practical and Natural Techniques That Will Improve Your Eyesight by Richard Leviton, 144 pages, paperback, $8.95

The Bread Book: A Natural, Whole-Grain Seed-to-Loaf Approach to Real Bread by Thom Leonard,110 pages, paperback, $8.95

Childbirth Wisdom: From the World's Oldest Societies by Judith Goldsmith, 291 pages, paperback, $10.95

Sweet and Natural Desserts: Wholesome, Sugar- and Dairy-Free Treats from the Editors of Natural Health, 120 pages, paperback, $8.95

Shopper's Guide to Natural Foods: A Consumer's Guide to Buying and Preparing Foods for Good Health from the Editors of Natural Health, 224 pages, paperback, $12.95

Meetings with Remarkable Men and Women from the Editors of Natural Health, 296 pages, paperback, $12.95

Fighting Radiation & Chemical Pollutants with Foods, Herbs, & Vitamins by Steven R. Schechter, N.D., 312 pages, paperback, $9.95

The Essential Movements of T'ai Chi by John Kostias, 169 pages, paperback, $11.95

Natural Childcare from the Editors of Natural Health, 216 pages, paperback, $10.95

Whole World Cookbook from the Editors of Natural Health, 140 pages, paperback, $6.95